THE CAREER
CHRONICLES

THE CAREER CHRONICLES

AN INSIDER'S GUIDE TO WHAT JOBS ARE REALLY LIKE

THE GOOD, THE BAD, AND

THE UGLY FROM OVER

750 PROFESSIONALS

Michael Gregory

New World Library
Novato, California

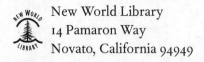 New World Library
14 Pamaron Way
Novato, California 94949

Text design by Tona Pearce Myers

Library of Congress Cataloging-in-Publication Data
Gregory, Michael (Michael G.)
The career chronicles : an insider's guide to what jobs are really like : the good, the bad, and the ugly from over 750 professionals / Michael Gregory.
    p.   cm.
ISBN 978-1-57731-573-5 (pbk. : alk. paper)
1. Vocational guidance. 2. Professions. 3. Occupations. I. Gregory, Michael. II. Title.
HF5382.G733 2008
331.702—dc22   2008004088

First printing, May 2008
ISBN: 978-1-57731-573-5

Printed in Canada on 100% postconsumer-waste recycled paper

New World Library is a proud member of the Green Press Initiative.

10 9 8 7 6 5 4 3 2 1

CONTENTS

A CAREER IN EDUCATION

CAREERS IN THE SOCIAL SCIENCES

A CAREER IN INFORMATION TECHNOLOGY

CAREERS IN SALES AND MARKETING

CAREERS IN GEOSCIENCE

CAREERS IN THE ARTS AND MEDIA

PREFACE

After several decades within the American work force, I was haunted by the fact that I hadn't selected the career path I truly wanted to follow.

By the time I was sixteen I had narrowed my choices to two: professional golfer and writer. I had made a hole-in-one at fifteen, so I just assumed that I had the natural talent to become the next Jack Nicklaus (this was long before Tiger Woods). What could be better — travel the world while making great money doing something I loved? Unfortunately, I was wrong about my level of talent. I never really elevated my golf game beyond my abilities as a fifteen-year-old, and I soon conceded that I was clearly not good enough to live off golf winnings.

So I shifted to my second choice — writing. It was also something I loved to do. The problem was that I didn't really know any writers, except through their writings. I had no one to talk to about writing, and no way to conceive what a career in writing was truly all about. I could have used a book like *The Career Chronicles*, with its hundreds of real-world observations of working life, but since I was unclear how to proceed, I abandoned writing as a career choice as well.

By the time I entered college, I was like millions of other college freshmen — I did not know in what direction I should proceed with my life. But I had at least eliminated some professions. Anything in the medical world was definitely not a viable option, as I was never excited by science. And like any narrow-minded son, I of course eliminated any professions my father had chosen, so there went a career in aviation or insurance. When it came time to select a major, I decided on economics. Unfortunately, by the time I graduated from college, I regrettably realized that a career as an economist promised to be rather dull. At least for me, graphs, charts, and statistical analyses were not enough to make me want to jump out of bed in the morning.

Like many other college students who had not yet found a satisfying career path, I decided to attend graduate school. Since one of my favorite books and movies as a child was *To Kill a Mockingbird*, I selected law school for my graduate studies. I would be like Gregory Peck's portrayal of Addicus Finch — dressed in a seersucker suit, a gold watch in my vest pocket, and with plenty of time for long, leisurely lunches and civic involvement. People would come to me with their problems, and I would dispense jewels of wisdom, for which they would be eternally grateful and would compensate me handsomely. My life would be orderly, socially meaningful, and intellectually fulfilling. Unfortunately, my Norman Rockwell image of the law back then was as far from reality as the plots and characters on the hit television show *Boston Legal* are today.

What I discovered was that the intellectual stimulation and fulfillment I had expected to find by practicing law were rapidly replaced by a stressful existence in which I had almost no control over my daily life. Instead of sitting at my desk dispensing jewels of legal wisdom or calmly researching the law in a quiet library, I was constantly being pulled in ten directions simultaneously.

I quickly learned that practicing law had two constants of which we as students were not fully apprised in law school. First, when people need the services of an attorney — whether for the sale or purchase of a business, the negotiation of a contract, a divorce, or a criminal matter — the issues they face are very critical to their personal or business lives. Clients arrive at a lawyer's doorstep only because they cannot finalize the matter to their own satisfaction by themselves, and they are being pressured by life, if they're not already in a crisis. Second, the procedural rules governing the legal profession, especially in the area of trial practice, are highly structured and time-sensitive. For an attorney, the net result is a work environment where all of your clients are anxious and competing for your limited time, and yet you are constantly having to rush from one matter to another so as to comply with all the procedural rules.

The more successful your practice, the more clients you acquire and the more intense the race to satisfy the pressing, competing demands of your clients and the law.

After two decades of court deadlines, demanding clients, late nights, working most weekends, missing too many important events in my children's lives, and rarely having an uninterrupted vacation, I decided to stop and instead pursue the dream I had been carrying with me since I was sixteen. I wanted to write for a living. I had always felt that writing could afford me the type of daily life that I now desperately longed for — the opportunity to be creative, to concentrate on one project at a time without endless interruptions, to experience the fulfillment of completing my own work, and to help others collectively, rather than one at a time, by producing works that engage and empower people.

Now that I have done this, I have found that I love my new career. Don't get me wrong. Writing isn't easy. The publishing world is a very tough business, and I have worked harder writing books than I have ever worked on anything else in my life. But for me there is something magical about it. I am constantly expanding my own knowledge and at the same time hopefully informing people and helping them reassess their lives and views. I enjoy my new work environment, too. I like that I can now literally work from anywhere, at my own pace, and listen to music while I am doing so.

I have always loved movies, and one scene from 1985's *Out of Africa* has stayed with me. In it, Robert Redford (portraying an English big-game hunter) tells Meryl Streep (who portrays his lover): "I don't want to come to the end of my life and realize I have lived someone else's version of it."

The secret for all of us is first to identify the version of the life we want to live, and then to not be afraid to live it.

INTRODUCTION

As we progress through high school and college, we are faced with one of the most important decisions of our lives: *What do I want to do with my life?*

Many students enter college without a clue what career or profession they should pursue. While at some point they must declare a major, this may not clarify their decision. Many change their major at least once, if not twice, thus extending the time it takes to graduate. Perhaps these individuals realize that the career they mapped out for themselves does not fit their goals, their personality, or their picture of the future. Others simply defer this pivotal life decision by escaping into graduate school, hoping that immersion in a particular field will provide them with the career direction they are seeking.

Others may have felt drawn to a particular profession early in their college life but find, after several years of real-world experience, that their initial image of their career does not match the realities. For millions of others, the need to reexamine their career choice is brought on by events beyond their control — such as mergers, acquisitions, downsizing, and restructuring — that eliminate their job, company, or even industry.

The bottom line is that at some point, and sometimes several, we will find ourselves facing a career choice. The more real-world, practical information we can gather about a particular profession, the better the chance our selection will be a good fit. This is what I am providing in *The Career Chronicles*, the type of detailed, practical, insider information we all need when facing a career decision.

The Career Chronicles presents helpful information from over 750 individuals in a wide variety of professions; although not completely comprehensive, these careers cover a wide spectrum of the types of opportunities available. Each part focuses on a broad employment category: health care, architecture and engineering, the law, accounting and financial services, education, the social sciences, computer technology, sales and marketing, geoscience, and the arts and media. Within these categories, major career types appear as separate chapters, and within these careers, interviewees reflect a range of even more specific career choices: both building and landscape architects, grade school teachers and high school teachers, and so on.

There are hundreds of different professions out there, so how did I end up with the ones in this book? I wanted to include a sufficiently broad array of careers that represented realistic opportunities for employment, but I did not want to cover so many careers that the book would take on an encyclopedic character and the reader would be bogged down in too much detail. I wanted *The Career Chronicles* to retain its candid and real-world tone and feel. Also, it was an evolving decision that to a large extent was dictated by the quantity and quality of responses I received from interviewees.

For example, I discovered that doctors are so busy they rarely had time to participate. So I elected not to include physicians in the health-care section, but I did incorporate nurses (a field that offers one of the greatest opportunities for job growth over the next decade), pharmacists (a well-paying career that is expanding as the baby-boomer population ages), dentists (another well-paying career that offers less of the stress that sometimes accompanies a doctor's practice), and veterinarians (whose treatments are approaching the level available to humans, in a country where there are more pets than people). Since health care is a major component of our economy, I also elected to include three professions from the social sciences that cross over to the world of health care in the broadest sense — psychologists, speech pathologists, and social workers or clinical therapists.

I also discovered that as we shift to a more environmentally conscious society within a world of declining natural resources, careers in geoscience have taken on a new importance, so I included geologist and soil scientist.

To provide a true comparison of professions, the format of each chapter is the same. This allows readers to easily compare one career with another. Each chapter begins with an instructive general and historical overview of the profession. This is followed with a summary (titled "By the Numbers") that presents the profession's educational and other requirements, the number of such professionals across the United States, and the average salary levels. "By the Numbers" frequently includes statistical data generated and maintained by the United States Bureau of Labor Statistics, representing the most up-to-date statistics available as of this book's publication in 2008.

The remainder of each chapter is devoted to the responses from professionals who agreed to be interviewed for this book. They provide commentary and real-world insight on their chosen careers or professions, and I've divided their feedback into six categories: "College vs. Reality," "The Biggest Surprise," "Hours and Advancement," "The Best and the Worst," "Changes in the Profession," and "Would You Do It All Over Again?"

These professionals hail from coast to coast and represent a broad range of experience and perspectives, but all provide candid, knowledgeable, lived advice. They are not trying to promote their professions with well-tailored marketing pitches. Rather, they provide personal observations about the good, the bad, and the ugly of each profession. To help keep the presentation of the information similar across professions

I posed the same questions to all the interviewees. Those questions include: "What are the best parts of your profession?" "What are the least enjoyable aspects of your profession?" "Have you found advancement within your career easy or difficult?" "What most surprised you about your chosen profession?" "Describe a typical day." "What changes do you foresee for your profession?" "Would you choose the same profession again?"

While doing the research for this book, I had the opportunity to interview or correspond with hundreds of Americans from all walks of life. Since I wanted to elicit truly candid responses, I agreed to not use the interviewees' names in the book. Instead, I have chosen to use a "semi-anonymous" format that provides some context for the reader: each quote is identified by the respondent's specific profession and how many years he or she has worked in the profession, and in what part of the United States.

The last chapter of *The Career Chronicles*, "Finding Your Dream Career," is dedicated to the proposition that if we follow our passion, the money will come and, even more importantly, the fulfillment we all seek in our daily lives will be present from the outset. In this final section, I present the comparative career choices of fifty individuals from across the country who were asked: "If you had all the money you needed, what career would you choose for your life?" Taking into account their current careers, you may find their answers both surprising and insightful.

CAREERS IN

Health Care

SO YOU WANT TO BE A NURSE

I thought there would be time for baths and foot rubs and lots of therapeutic listening. Looking back, I realize how naïve that expectation was. The reality of nursing is caring for individuals experiencing a crisis in their life, acute exacerbations of a chronic disease, or disease and injuries that require medical interventions. The health-care industry is complex, confusing, and often intimidating to patients and their families. The language is incomprehensible to many, and the procedures, treatments, and often even the medications are alien to laypeople. They want to ask questions and feel empowered to participate in the decisions but many times must look to the nurses, doctors, and often unskilled assistants to interpret events and choices. I was not prepared for the degree of trust I often feel patients and families grant others as well as myself involved in their care.

Although nursing dates back to the fifteenth century or earlier, when women were regularly hired to take care of the newborn children of other women, most people associate the origin of the nursing profession with one name — Florence Nightingale. Born in 1820 to wealthy English parents while they were touring Europe, she was named after the city of her birth — Florence, Italy. Starting when she was sixteen, Nightingale reported hearing the voice of God calling her to do his work, although at the time she did not know what that work would involve. From 1949 to 1950, Nightingale toured Egypt and Europe, where she began her training as a nurse, first in Egypt and then in Germany. That trip would change her life — and the profession of nursing. In 1853 she took a position as superintendent of the Institute for the Care of Sick Gentlewomen in London.

In 1854, Britain, France, and Turkey declared war on Russia. During what was known as the Crimean War, Florence Nightingale was asked to introduce female nurses into the military hospitals in Turkey. The experiment was an outstanding success, and after the war, the "Lady-in-Chief," as she was referred to, established the Nightingale Training School for Nurses and authored the book *Notes on Nursing*, which was translated into eleven languages and is still in print today. Until her death at age ninety, Florence Nightingale devoted the rest of her life to improving health standards and advancing nursing as a respectable profession for women, publishing two hundred books, reports, and pamphlets. In 1872, at the New England Hospital for Women and Children in Boston, the first formal training school for nurses in the United States opened its doors.

In the broadest sense, as a profession or career, nursing focuses on maintaining optimal health for individuals, families, and communities. There are a number of different educational paths to a nursing career, yet all involve a combination of the study of nursing theory and training in clinical skills. Students learn a "nursing process" to assess and diagnose needs, to implement interventions, and to continually evaluate outcomes of the care. The American Nurses Association defines nursing as "the protection, promotion, and optimization of health and abilities; prevention of illness and injury; alleviation of suffering through the diagnosis and treatment of human responses; and advocacy in health care for individuals, families, communities, and populations." Nursing is the most diverse of all health-care professions, with over seventy-five different recognized specializations within the field, including *pediatric nursing, obstetrics-gynecology nursing, neonatal nursing, geriatric nursing, psychiatric and mental health nursing, oncology nursing, emergency nursing, critical care nursing, intensive care nursing, surgical nursing, radiology nursing, orthopedic nursing, public health nursing, hospice nursing, holistic nursing, home-health nursing,* and *nursing instruction.*

According to the U.S. Bureau of Labor Statistics, *registered nurses* constitute the largest health-care occupation in the country, with over 2.5 million jobs. A registered nurse is defined as "a graduate trained nurse who has passed a state administered national registration examination, and has been licensed to practice nursing." The National Council Licensure Examination–Registered Nurse (NCLEX-RN) is a standardized test presented in a multiple-choice, fill-in-the-blank, and area-identification format, which tests current medical knowledge and nursing competencies within a "Meeting the Patient's Needs" framework.

To achieve the position of registered nurse, there are three possible educational paths: a Bachelor of Science Degree in Nursing (BSN), an Associate Degree in Nursing (ADN), or a hospital Diploma of Nursing. As of 2006, there were 709 BSN programs (which traditionally take four years to complete) available through colleges and universities in the United States. The BSN curriculum includes courses on physical assessment, disease management, clinical decision making, health promotion and prevention, health-care technology, health-care policy, research, quality assurance, leadership, and management. In addition, a clinical component, comprising hospital work as well as possibly working in patients' homes, school-based clinics, and adult living communities, is a major part of the curriculum.

During the same year, approximately 850 ADN programs in the United States offered associate degrees (which traditionally take two to three years to complete), while approximately 70 hospitals in the United States administered Diploma of Nursing programs. In addition, to serve the needs of RNs with an associate degree or a nursing diploma who want to secure a Bachelor of Science in Nursing, in 2006 there were 629 RN-to-BSN programs available. There were also multiple Master of Science in Nursing (MSN) programs as well as 149 RN-to-MSN programs in the United States.

In addition to registered nurses, the world of nursing offers the position of *licensed practical nurse* (LPN), which is defined in the *American Heritage Medical Dictionary* as "an individual who has completed a practical nursing program, and is licensed by a state to provide routine patient care under the direction of a registered nurse or a physician." Most yearlong practical nursing programs (for which a high school diploma is usually required) include both classroom study and supervised clinical practice (patient care). As of 2006, there were 1,500 LPN programs in the United States. To obtain licensure as an LPN, one must pass the NCLEX-PN licensing exam administered by the National Council of State Boards of Nursing.

For a successful nursing career, a caring, sympathetic nature is almost a must. Good observation and communication skills are pluses, as is being able to work as part of a team. On a day-to-day basis, nurses assist and care for sick and injured people, and the environment is often emotional and stressful as patients become confused and agitated. In addition, nurses can be exposed to caustic chemicals, radiation, and infectious diseases. However, for those individuals who like to help others, nursing can be one of the most rewarding careers available.

Nurses continue to be in strong demand, and there are currently more positions available than individuals to fill them. As a result, wages continue to rise, and hospitals and other employers often offer sign-on bonuses and flexible work hours. According to the latest data from the U.S. Bureau of Labor Statistics, between 2006 and 2016, there will be over 500,000 new positions available for registered nurses, as the baby-boomer generation reaches retirement age and as a substantial percentage of the existing nursing population retires. This represents one of the largest numbers of projected new jobs among all occupations tracked by the Bureau of Labor Statistics.

BY THE NUMBERS

EMPLOYMENT LEVELS: The latest available data from the U.S. Bureau of Labor Statistics report over 2.5 million registered nurses in the country, of which 59 percent work in hospitals and 21 percent work part-time. There is currently a nationwide shortage of registered nurses, and demand is expected to remain high for at least the next decade, with physician's offices, home health-care services, and outpatient care centers creating the most new positions.

ACADEMIC REQUIREMENTS: To become a registered nurse, one can complete either a four-year Bachelor of Nursing program, a two- to three-year Associate of Nursing program, or a three-year Hospital Diploma program, and then must pass the NCLEX-RN, a national standardized examination administered by the National Council of State Boards of Nursing.

AVERAGE SALARY LEVELS: According to the U.S. Bureau of Labor Statistics, the annual median earnings for registered nurses are **$57,820**, within a salary range of **$40,250** to **$83,440**. The online career advancement resource Salary.com reports that the current nationwide median salary for registered nurses is **$59,859**, and for licensed practical nurses, the nationwide median salary is **$38,189**.

COLLEGE VS. REALITY

How would you compare the reality of your profession to the picture you had of it while in school?

I thought there would be time for baths and foot rubs and lots of therapeutic listening. Looking back, I realize how naïve that expectation was. The reality of nursing is caring for individuals experiencing a crisis in their life, acute exacerbations of a chronic disease, or disease and injuries that require medical interventions. The health-care industry is complex, confusing, and often intimidating to patients and their families. The language is incomprehensible to many, and the procedures, treatments, and often even the medications are alien to laypeople. They want to ask questions and feel empowered to participate in the decisions but many times must look to the nurses, doctors, and often unskilled assistants to interpret events and choices. I was not prepared for the degree of trust I often feel patients and families grant others as well as myself involved in their care.

—Registered nurse, 16 years,
Longview, Texas

I was not prepared for the paper compliance. That was thirty-four years ago. Little did I know, health-care regulations (in long-term care, in particular) are unreal. Regulations in long-term care are second only to those in nuclear power plants.

—Nursing administrator in geriatrics,
34 years, Ephrata, Pennsylvania

Pretty much what you see is what you get. In nursing school you actually work numerous clinical rotations. During those, you simply work every day on the floor as a nurse with your own patient load and everything. The only thing is that you are supervised by a regular nurse there, and you don't get paid for it. Once you graduate, you continue doing the same basic thing, only then you can finally draw a paycheck for doing it. Still, there are a million different areas that

you could work in, such as OR [operating room], ICU [intensive care unit], ER [emergency room], oncology, pediatrics, doctors' offices, schools, et cetera, et cetera, so they can't get you experience in all of them, but the main ones, yeah, you pretty much know what to expect.

—Registered nurse, 15 years,
Carrollton, Texas

. . .

How would you rate your collegiate and graduate courses in preparing you for your profession on a scale of 1 to 10, with 10 being the best?

7 out of 10. The core curriculum provided a solid foundation. Instructors made many of the classes stressful, which was a good obstacle to deal with due to the stress in the real world upon graduation.

—Occupational therapist, 12 years,
Farmerville, Louisiana

An 8. I had good instructors and a good mix of clinical training.

—Registered nurse, 6 years,
Gainesville, Florida

The reality of nursing is that you do not receive enough training. Nursing schools do their best to present nursing as "peachy."

—Registered nurse, 5 years,
Bossier City, Louisiana

THE BIGGEST SURPRISE

What most surprised you about your chosen profession?

The high demand for nurses and the wide variety of job options that it accordingly affords you.

—Psychiatric nurse, 16 years,
Long Beach, California

The lack of helping each other to make the job easier.

—Registered nurse, 8 years,
Caddo Parish, Louisiana

Nurses complain . . . a lot!

—Registered nurse, 10 years,
Petaluma, California

HOURS AND ADVANCEMENT

How many hours do you work each week at your career?

Forty.

—Registered nurse, 8 years,
Greenville, South Carolina

Thirty-six — three twelve-hour shifts.

—Registered nurse, 16 years,
Nashville, Tennessee

Fifty to fifty-two.

—Registered nurse, 22 years,
Lancaster, Pennsylvania

. . .

Have you found advancement within your career easy or difficult?

Easy if you want to be a manager, but I have no desire to be in a management position.

—Operating room nurse, 17 years,
San Diego, California

Easy. There is a nursing shortage, and good nurses can advance quickly.

—Registered nurse, 7 years,
Richmond, Virginia

Easy.

—Registered nurse, 14 years,
Independence, Missouri

THE BEST AND THE WORST

What do you spend most of your day doing? Describe a typical day.

My current position is in preadmission testing. I see patients who will be having surgery within one to two weeks. My responsibility is to assess patients and teach them about the procedure, the care they will receive at the hospital, and how they are to care for themselves at home. I ensure that the appropriate testing is done according to the surgeon's orders and consult with the anesthesiologist regarding tests required based on the physical assessment. I confirm that the appropriate diagnosis is documented for each test done. I contact outside resources for those patients who have specific needs. I see up to eight patients a day.

—Registered nurse, 39 years, Coldwater, Ohio

I get to work, change from my street clothes into scrubs, and don a nametag. I get a report on my patients for the day and go meet them. I find out what they will need by reading their doctor's orders and by what I hear from my report. Then I assess the patient or patients. If I am working with a labor patient, I only have one patient at a time. Well, really there are two if you count the fetus. If I am working in adult ICU, I have one or two patients concurrently. If I am working in post-partum, I have up to four mom-and-baby couplets; that is really eight patients. After initial assessments, I do the necessary things for my patient grouping. When a baby is born, there is a huge amount of work to help mom and baby recover. Mom can bleed if the uterus isn't behaving, and babies can transition poorly to extrauterine life and need close watching. In the ICU, there are many complex and layered assessments to make. There are a huge number of machines used there, so the mechanics are as important as the human interaction. I call doctors or work with them directly with patients. I manage a lot of equipment and use my people skills concurrently. There is a lot of communication, teaching, and comforting that goes on constantly throughout the day. There are whole families who also become my patients, as the real patient isn't the only one who needs caring for. Sometimes the family is the biggest challenge of my day, for instance if the loved one is dying and I need to counsel the family about all the available options in a language they can understand. At the end of a shift, I give a report to the next shift, and then I go home. Hopefully, I have had time for a thirty-minute meal break and a couple of ten-minute breathers. Most often I get the meal break, but the others are really just two minutes to go to the bathroom and drink some water.

—Registered nurse, 25 years, Petaluma, California

On a typical day, I care for four patients. My day may include giving medications (oral and IV), doing several head-to-toe assessments of patients, starting IVs, drawing blood for lab work, helping patients walk in the halls, doing skin care and changing dressings, educating patients about their disease process, completing lots of paperwork, communicating with patients' families, and much more.

—Acute care registered nurse, 2 years, Portland, Oregon

. . .

What are the best parts of your profession?

Working in a caring profession, and the high salary.

—Psychiatric technician, 16 years,
Long Beach, California

Making a real difference in people's lives.

—Registered nurse, 14 years,
Bethesda, Maryland

Knowing that my job is an essential one, and one for which I am well paid.

—Emergency room nurse, 11 years,
Charlotte, North Carolina

. . .

What are the least enjoyable aspects of your profession?

When there is nothing we can do to make someone better.

—Registered nurse, 3 years,
Shreveport, Louisiana

The exposure to infectious diseases.

—Licensed practical nurse, 3 years,
Lincoln, Nebraska

Dealing with the emotions of families who do not understand or fail to come to grips with the reality of the condition of a patient.

—Intensive care unit nurse, 21 years,
Rockford, Illinois

CHANGES IN THE PROFESSION

What changes do you foresee for your profession?

Hopefully more nurses, and more well-rounded nurses who are geared more toward being clinicians. Also a better understanding of narcotics and their true purpose, and to not be afraid of patient addiction when patients are desperately in need of good pain control. There are higher expectations for nurses these days as a result of having to keep up with the ever-changing pharmacology and technology.

—Nursing instructor and hospice nurse,
20 years, Long Beach, California

An increase in technology, and a decrease in holistic care.

—Nursing director, 15 years,
Webster Parish, Louisiana

Direct third-party reimbursement for nurses has been a dream of my professors' and mine since the early 1980s, but I don't know if it will happen. I'd like to anticipate positive changes, but so much is driven by money. Hopefully the heart of nursing — the passion we have for helping people when they are the most vulnerable — will always survive. I know for sure the bulk of our workforce will be retiring in ten to twenty years (I'm one of them), many have already left the profession due to burnout, and nursing programs don't have enough teachers to teach the numbers of nurses needed.

—Registered nurse, 26 years,
Stillwater, Minnesota

WOULD YOU DO IT ALL OVER AGAIN?

Do you find your daily job fulfilling?

Yes. It's nice to help others in their quest toward wellness. Where each individual lands on that spectrum varies, but we're always trying to move them along the continuum. Aiding and assisting others is very rewarding. We all need each other in this journey called life.

—Registered nurse and
occupational health manager, 29 years,
Brea, California

Some days are fulfilling, such as when we do an organ transplant and give a person a new lease on life. Some days not, such as when I had to fix the broken ankle of a drunk driver who had just killed a family in a motor vehicle accident.

—Registered nurse, 17 years,
San Diego, California

Without a doubt! There are days when exhaustion and disappointment and sorrow can color your world with a darkness that hurts. But then you return; you continue to pursue excellence for the best outcome; and through your work, you are uplifted and encouraged and supported to return and continue the jobs that need to be done. When a family smiles, a baby settles in, a surgery goes well, a baby improves, a grandparent says thank you, a small hand grabs yours, that is all we need to know that we are doing work that is special, important, and life-changing. That is what helps our hearts feel very full.

—Neonatal intensive care unit registered
nurse, 28 years, Costa Mesa, California

. . .

Would you choose the same profession again?

Yes — I enjoy making a difference in people's lives.

—Registered nurse, 10 years,
Shreveport, Louisiana

Yes. The job is rewarding, the pay is great, and the hours are quite flexible. Plus you can do many different things with this career.

—Registered nurse, 10 years,
Petaluma, California

No. There is too much beyond my control.

—Registered nurse, 16 years,
Bossier Parish, Louisiana

SO YOU WANT TO BE A PHARMACIST

The best things about being a pharmacist are helping others in need, receiving a patient's respect when he or she realizes what a valuable resource a pharmacist is, and the patients who come to me with health-related questions, sometimes even before seeking advice from their physicians. It gives me great joy to help those people, and to build strong relationships with them.

It can be argued that pharmacy began when the first caveman used cool water, a leaf, and mud to soothe the pain from a cut or abrasion. The first record of the practice of pharmacy comes from Babylon in 2600 BC; the Chinese were using herbs for medicinal purposes as far back as 2000 BC. The oldest preserved medical document, *Papyrus Ebers*, came from Egypt and dates to around 1552 BC. This 110-page scroll contains seven hundred different formulas and remedies and is believed by some scholars to be a copy of the even more ancient works of Thoth (circa 3000 BC), who is the reputed father of medicine and pharmacy.

The word "pharmacy" is derived from the Greek word for "drug," and it was advances in ancient Middle Eastern botany and chemistry that led to the development of the science of pharmacology. Today, the profession of pharmacy acts as the link between the health sciences and the chemical sciences.

In the United States, the first college of pharmacy was founded in 1822 in Philadelphia, when sixty-eight apothecaries met to improve scientific standards and professional training. The curriculum emphasized the biological and chemical sciences, including bacteriology, biology, and chemistry. Now known as the University of the Sciences in Philadelphia, the Philadelphia College of Pharmacy launched the careers of many of the innovative pioneers in the health-care field, including the founders of some of the world's leading pharmaceutical companies, such as Dr. Eli Lilly (Eli Lilly and Company) and William R. Warner (Warner-Lambert Company, which later merged with Pfizer).

Just as the profession of pharmacy acts as the link between the health sciences and the chemical sciences, the pharmacist acts as a link between important groups in the world of health care — between physician and patient (as the dispenser of medications), and between pharmaceutical companies and consumers.

As with all health-care professions, the pharmacist's principal goal is to improve the health of the patient — by curing, slowing, or preventing disease; by eliminating or reducing symptoms; and by achieving desired changes in the patient's physiological processes. Pharmacists focus on and become experts in medicines and drugs and so must be highly knowledgeable about the composition of drugs, their chemical and physical properties, and their manufacture and use, as well as how to test for purity and strength. Pharmacists must understand the purpose of each drug and how it works within the human body — its benefits, side effects, and dangers.

In the United States, every state and the District of Columbia require a license to become a practicing pharmacist. To obtain a license, you must graduate from an accredited college of pharmacy and then pass the North American Pharmacist Licensure Exam (NAPLEX). In addition, forty-three states and the District of Columbia require that you pass the Multistate Pharmacy Jurisprudence Exam (MPJE), which tests pharmacy law. There are over eighty accredited colleges of pharmacy in the United States that award a doctor of pharmacy degree, which requires six years of postsecondary study; most programs also require a year or more of hands-on training in conjunction with practicing pharmacists. Students who like and perform well in mathematics and the natural sciences (such as chemistry, biology, and physics) may want to consider a career as a pharmacist. Also, if the financial and time commitment to become a doctor seems overwhelming, becoming a pharmacist offers a career in the medical world with a shorter, and accordingly less expensive, academic route to actual practice.

The world of science is continuously making advancements in the treatment of disease, which in turn requires pharmacists to keep abreast of the latest drug therapies and drug interactions. And today the American medical establishment is also evolving, and pharmacists are expected to play a more integral part in the health-care system beyond just the historical role of formulating and dispensing medication.

One example of this expanded role is the increased number of clinical pharmacists, who provide patient care that optimizes the use of medication and promotes wellness and disease prevention. The clinical pharmacy movement began inside hospitals and clinics, but it is expanding to the neighborhood pharmacy. As a result, many pharmacists elect to secure advanced degrees and become board-certified as *oncology pharmacists*, *psychiatric pharmacists*, and other specialists, such as *nuclear pharmacists*. Nuclear pharmacy refers to the compounding and dispensing of radioactive material for use in nuclear medical procedures, which encompass treatments involving radioactive substances, radionuclide imaging, and nuclear scintigraphy. Also, pharmacists are central to the explosive growth of "in-store walk-in convenient-care clinics." In our time-pressed society, pharmacy chains see a big business in treating minor medical matters directly, and it's becoming increasingly routine for pharmacists to work in conjunction with other medical personnel inside the walls of your neighborhood drugstore.

The future of pharmacy as a career looks bright. In particular, with the American baby-boomer generation currently reaching retirement age, the demand for pharmaceuticals will only increase. The major drugstore chains have expansive plans — seemingly to build a neighborhood pharmacy on almost every corner — and every single one of these retail facilities will require pharmacists to operate and manage them. Pharmacists will also continue to play an integral role in every setting in the health-care world: in hospitals, clinics, and other health-care facilities; as part of the home health-care industry; as researchers for pharmaceutical companies; as advisors for health insurance companies; and as members or directors of public health-care service agencies.

BY THE NUMBERS

EMPLOYMENT LEVELS: According to the U.S. Bureau of Labor Statistics, pharmacists hold approximately 230,000 positions in the United States, with 60 percent working in community pharmacies, and 24 percent working in hospitals and clinics. Pharmacists also work for home-health agencies, for pharmaceutical manufacturers developing new drugs, for health insurance companies developing benefit packages, and for the government and public health-care services.

ACADEMIC REQUIREMENTS: To practice as a licensed pharmacist, you must graduate from an accredited college of pharmacy (as designated by the Accreditation Council of Pharmacy Education) and pass the NAPLEX (North American Pharmacist Licensure Exam). The majority of states also require that prospective pharmacists pass the MPJE (Multistate Pharmacy Jurisprudence Exam), which tests pharmacy law. A doctor of pharmacy degree requires at least six years of postsecondary education. Pharmacy graduates can also become certified in such specialties as oncology, nuclear pharmacy, pharmacology, and psychiatric pharmacy.

AVERAGE SALARY LEVELS: According to the American Pharmacy Association, the median salary for an entry-level pharmacist is **$75,300**, while that of a pharmacy manager is **$93,100**. Neither figure includes a sign-on bonus, which is becoming more common.

COLLEGE VS. REALITY

How would you compare the reality of your profession to the picture you had of it while in school?

From the nature of the course and study structure in obtaining a degree in pharmacy, which includes a large amount of on-the-job training, I entered the world of a retail pharmacy with a real view of what lay ahead.

—Retail pharmacist, 8 years,
Rockford, Illinois

Being a practicing pharmacist is very much as I pictured it, yet the critical nature of the job and the desire to be thorough in your understanding of the side effects and drug-disease interactions can only be fully appreciated once you are doing it on a daily basis.

—Clinical pharmacist, 4 years,
Louisville, Kentucky

One important aspect of being an effective pharmacist centers on keeping abreast of new drugs that are being developed and their impact in disease management. I did not fully appreciate the impact of that portion of the job until I began having my own repeat customers.

—Retail pharmacist, 2 years,
Middletown, Ohio

. . .

How would you rate your collegiate and graduate courses in preparing

you for your profession on a scale of 1 to 10, with 10 being the best?

9–10. Several of my professors were also practicing pharmacists and taught courses in their specialty. Their continuing participation as active pharmacists in either a university clinic or a retail setting translated well in preparing us to enter the profession.

—**Retail pharmacist, 5 years,
Paterson, New Jersey**

An 8 or 9. The nature of the curriculum and the makeup of the professors (many of whom have been active pharmacists) combine to provide a very good overview of the nature of a pharmacy practice.

—**Hospital pharmacist, 7 years,
Newport News, Virginia**

An 8. Courses can only teach so much about dealing with the public and their emotions and peculiarities.

—**Retail pharmacist, 12 years,
Gainesville, Florida**

THE BIGGEST SURPRISE

What most surprised you about your chosen profession?

The emotional intensity of disgruntled customers when they think the health-care system or the insurance companies are not treating them fairly. Some people can really be difficult to deal with.

—**Retail pharmacist, 6 years, Longview, Texas**

How the demand for pharmacists continues to grow at such a rapid rate. It was this way when I entered the profession, but I felt that it would have to slow down, and yet it has continued unabated.

—**Clinical pharmacist, 8 years,
Augusta, Georgia**

How many new drugs are being developed. The pace of drug development has been surprising, even for someone so connected to the industry, and requires that we maintain an ongoing reassessment of new medications and the latest in disease management.

—**Retail pharmacist, 11 years,
Aurora, Colorado**

HOURS AND ADVANCEMENT

How many hours do you work each week at your career?

The hours that one works as a pharmacist is one of the pluses of the job. It rarely exceeds forty hours.

—**Retail pharmacist, 5 years,
Scottsdale, Arizona**

Forty to forty-four.

—**Hospital pharmacist, 14 years,
Tallahassee, Florida**

I am currently working a blend of twelve-hour shifts and eight-hour shifts, so it varies from week to week, but usually falls within the window of forty to forty-eight hours.

—Retail pharmacist, 10 years,
Mt. Pleasant, South Carolina

. . .

Have you found advancement within your career easy or difficult?

Our profession is unlike most professions. It does not really provide a set avenue for advancement. The duties are virtually the same for all pharmacists regardless of the number of years one has been in the profession. However, one can increase their salary and their responsibilities by becoming certified in a variety of specialties, such as nuclear pharmacy.

—Retail pharmacist, 9 years,
Rockville, Maryland

Advancement in the pharmacy world used to mean buying into, as a partner, your own drugstore. However, the day of the self-owned store is almost over, as the corporate chains seemingly open a new store on almost every corner. Opportunities do exist for those with entrepreneurial interests to own their own pharmacy practice within the retail entity of a larger company.

—Retail pharmacist, 13 years,
Spokane, Washington

The only real advancement track in most pharmacies is taking on a managerial role, but with it comes the responsibilities and headaches of being a pharmacy manager, such as overseeing and being accountable for the operational and financial results of the pharmacy. With certain national companies, there is also the opportunity to increase income by becoming a regional pharmacy manager, which brings on even more managerial duties, including recruiting pharmacists and overseeing compliance with all governmental regulations.

—Retail pharmacist, 18 years, Irving, Texas

THE BEST AND THE WORST

What do you spend most of your day doing? Describe a typical day.

My day is a mix of interpreting doctors' orders, filling prescriptions, cross-checking for drug-to-drug and drug-to-disease reactions, answering questions from patients as regards their concerns about dosage, proper usage, and side effects with medication, explaining to customers the application of certain over-the-counter medications, and dealing with insurance companies, with the majority of my time filling prescriptions.

—Retail pharmacist, 3 years,
Macon, Georgia

My days are varied as to what receives the most attention, but during any given week I have to attend to matters involving product purchasing, operational matters, employee scheduling, hiring and firing, marketing, supervising the pharmacists that work under me, and insurance payment issues.

—Retail pharmacy store manager, 15 years,
Lowell, Massachusetts

My days in the hospital pharmacy are centered around the constant of operating efficient systems for controlling drug distribution, so as to assure that each patient receives the appropriate medication, in the correct form and dosage, at the correct time. I spend my days maintaining accurate records to achieve this goal and to assist in screening for drug allergies and adverse effects.

—Hospital pharmacist, 11 years,
Cincinnati, Ohio

. . .

What are the best parts of your profession?

The excellent job opportunities. Due to the fact that more baby-boomers are living longer and will need health care for a longer period of time, the outlook for the pharmaceutical industry is quite bright now and into the future. The demand for pharmacists, as the professionals who are the connection between the heath-care consumer and the pharmaceutical companies, has never been greater. A licensed pharmacist can pretty much name the city where he or she would like to work, and many times there will be a sign-on bonus in addition to a competitive salary.

—Retail pharmacist, 3 years,
Modesto, California

I work as a pharmacist for a large national retail chain. One of the pluses of my job is the fact that when my shift ends, I do not have to take my work home with me. Whether you are working an eight-hour shift or a twelve-hour shift, or rotating from one to the other, when your day ends, you can leave your work issues pretty much behind you. That may not be the case if you owned your own pharmacy, but those settings are becoming fewer and farther between in this country.

—Retail pharmacist, 10 years,
Norman, Oklahoma

The best things about being a pharmacist are helping others in need, receiving a patient's respect when he or she realizes what a valuable resource a pharmacist is, and the patients who come to me with health-related questions, sometimes even before seeking advice from their physicians. It gives me great joy to help those people, and to build strong relationships with them. When I first started working as a pharmacist, I quickly became friends with an elderly gentleman whose wife was battling cancer. With each and every new drug his wife was taking, he always asked my opinion, wanting to know the side effects he should expect. Sadly, after a year, his wife lost her battle with cancer. I will never forget the day he walked into the pharmacy, just to let me know that she had passed away, and to thank me for my help. Several months after her death, my customer brought me a copy of a poem his wife had written before her death. I proudly display that poem in my home.

—Retail pharmacist, 2 years,
Brentwood, Tennessee

...

What are the least enjoyable aspects of your profession?

Dealing with customers' emotions. Quite often pharmacists catch the brunt of people's frustration about health insurance coverage and which drugs are paid for and which are not.

—Retail pharmacist, 7 years,
Bowling Green, Kentucky

Dealing with insurance companies. This part of the job is disliked by everyone in the health-care field, and pharmacists are no exception.

—Retail pharmacist, 5 years,
Asheville, North Carolina

The emphasis by the major retail drug chains on how many prescriptions are filled rather than on building long-term relationships with customers.

—Retail pharmacist, 3 years,
Arlington, Virginia

CHANGES IN THE PROFESSION

What changes do you foresee for your profession?

The entire atmosphere of the pharmacy experience in America has been permanently altered by the corporate dominance of an industry that once comprised pharmacists who were also small-business owners, members of their community, and your neighbors. This corporate dominance will only continue and will begin to incorporate on a national scale the addition of the walk-in clinic for the assessment and treatment of minor family medical issues.

—Retail pharmacist, 24 years,
Jackson, Mississippi

There will be continued growth in the managed-care pharmacy, where managed-care pharmacists play a more pivotal role in disease management programs.

—Retail pharmacist, 7 years,
Piscataway, New Jersey

As more and more new drugs are being developed, pharmacists will be required to spend more and more time keeping abreast of the new drugs, the drug-to-drug interactions, side effects, and the expanding aspects of disease management.

—Hospital pharmacist, 11 years, Topeka, Kansas

WOULD YOU DO IT ALL OVER AGAIN?

Do you find your daily job fulfilling?

Yes. All in all the positives outweigh the negatives. I am in a field that is always being updated, thus challenging me academically, and I am in a profession that allows me to assist people in one of the most crucial areas of their lives.

—Retail pharmacist, 15 years, Eugene, Oregon

At times I do feel somewhat odd about my job, as I work nights in one corner of a huge grocery store, in between the bakery and the canned goods. It has such a retail atmosphere to it that you sometimes lose your identity in the health-care world.

—Retail pharmacist, 4 years, Shreveport, Louisiana

Yes, I do. I know that I am helping people with issues that cause them great concern. I am many times the front-line liaison and communicator between the patients and the health-care system. They don't need an appointment to seek my advice. I pride myself on being approachable and patient.

—Retail pharmacist, 12 years, Livonia, Michigan

. . .

Would you choose the same profession again?

Yes, I would. I was able to elect what city I cared to practice in, and I am paid well for my time. The stress is low compared to many other fields in the health-care system.

—Hospital pharmacist, 6 years, Virginia Beach, Virginia

Yes, but I would work in a hospital pharmacy, where the hours are better, and I remain in a learning and teaching environment. The retail world is so profit driven that I sometimes feel more like a salesman than a medical professional.

—Retail pharmacist, 8 years, Rome, Georgia

I knew I wanted to work in the health-care system. I could help others, and the pay was going to be superior to that in most other fields. I did not want to have the long hours of a physician, and dentistry simply did not interest me, so pharmacy was a happy medium. I would choose it again.

—Clinical pharmacist, 2 years, Huntsville, Alabama

SO YOU WANT TO BE A DENTIST

It can be a huge investment to start up a dental practice, and even if you do not hang out your own shingle but rather start as an associate in an existing practice, ultimately you are going to be involved in a wide range of business- and employment-related issues. With that in mind, I wish I had taken a few more business courses along the way.

Most people do not get excited about a trip to the dentist; at best, someone pushes, scrapes, and pulls inside our mouths, and at worst, out comes the drill. Indeed, we have had a love-hate relationship with dentistry for thousands of years: until we have a problem, we avoid dentists like the plague, but when pain arrives or we break a tooth, we rush to dentists like they are saviors sent from heaven.

Hesy-Re, an Egyptian scribe who is often referred to as the first dentist, died around 2600 BC, and on his tomb is the inscription "the greatest of those who deal with teeth, and of physicians." Between 500 and 300 BC, Hippocrates and Aristotle wrote about dentistry, including the eruption pattern of teeth, treating decayed teeth and gum disease, extracting teeth, and using wires to stabilize loose teeth and jaws. Monks practiced dentistry during the early Middle Ages in Europe, while a medical text in China from about the year 700 refers to the use of a "silver paste," a type of amalgam. In 1530, *The Little Medicinal Book for All Kinds of Diseases and Infirmities of the Teeth* by Artzney Buchlein was published in Germany. French surgeon Pierre Fauchard is known as the father of modern dentistry because his 1723 book, *The Surgeon Dentist, A Treatise on Teeth*, was the first to describe a comprehensive system for practicing dentistry, including basic oral anatomy and function, operative and restorative techniques, and denture construction.

In the United States, one of America's first dentists was Paul Revere. In 1776 he conducted what is considered the first case of postmortem dental forensics when he verified the death of his friend Dr. Joseph Warren, during the Revolutionary War battle of Breed's Hill, by identifying the bridge he had constructed for Dr. Warren. The world's first dental school, the Baltimore College of Dental Surgery, was founded in 1840, and the American Dental Association was formed in 1859. The first dental X-ray was taken by New Orleans dentist C. Edmond Kells in 1895. Edward Hartley Angle created the dental specialty of orthodontics in 1899. In 1943, Colorado dentist Frederick S. McKay discovered the beneficial connection between fluoride levels in water and lower cavity rates. By 1960, lasers had been developed and approved for soft-tissue procedures. The use of dental implants began during the 1980s. Most recently, the use of tooth-colored restorative materials and the increased use of bleaching, veneers, and implants have inaugurated an era of aesthetic, or cosmetic, dentistry, which continues to grow throughout the United States.

Yet dentistry is about much more than beautiful smiles and enhanced appearances. Dentistry is on the cutting edge of broader medical issues as well, such as molecular-based and "lab-on-a-chip" oral cancer detection techniques. Dentists are also involved in patient research with applications across broader medical lines, such as protein profiling and gene therapy. And as practitioners, dentists are also entrepreneurs who must manage a business with multiple employees; these could include dental hygienists, dental assistants, dental lab technicians, bookkeepers, and receptionists.

While most dentists are general practitioners, others elect to enter various specialty areas. These include *orthodonists* (who straighten teeth), *oral and maxillofacial surgeons* (who operate on the mouth and jaws), *pediatric dentists* (who focus on dentistry for children), *periodontists* (who treat gums and bone supporting the teeth), *endodontists* (who perform root canal therapy), *prosthodontists* (who replace missing teeth with permanent fixtures, such as crowns and bridges, or with removable fixtures, such as dentures), *oral pathologists* (who study oral diseases), and *dental radiologists* (who diagnose diseases in the head and neck with imaging technology).

Those interested in dentistry have to be ready to make a long-term academic commitment. While not as long as the path through medical school, internship, and residency, dental school lasts four years, and this is traditionally commenced after completion of a Bachelor of Science degree, preferably with a concentration in biology or chemistry. In dental school, classroom instruction and laboratory work include such courses as anatomy, microbiology, biochemistry, and physiology. The last two years are usually devoted to clinical instruction and actual work in dental clinics associated with the dental college itself. If one's desire is to enter a dental specialty, it can take an additional two to five years, depending on the specialty. All states require that dentists be licensed.

The country has fifty-six accredited dental schools, and dental graduates must pass written and practical examinations before they can apply for a license to practice. The written portion of each state's licensing requirement can be fulfilled by passing the National Board Dental Examinations, administered by the individual states or regional testing agencies. Most licensed graduates become employees of dental practices with established client bases; over time, they may have the opportunity to become partners in the practice. Or dentists negotiate to purchase on some agreed-on installment basis the practice of a dentist who is ready to retire.

BY THE NUMBERS

EMPLOYMENT LEVELS: According to the U.S. Bureau of Labor Statistics, there are 150,000 dentists in the United States, of which 128,000 practice general dentistry. The largest group of dental specialists is orthodontists, followed by oral and maxillofacial surgeons.

ACADEMIC REQUIREMENTS: To practice dentistry, you must graduate from one of the nation's fifty-six dental schools accredited by the American Dental Association. The dental school program lasts four years, with the last two focusing on clinical training. A dental specialty — such as for orthodontists, periodontists, and endodontists — can take two to five years of additional education.

AVERAGE SALARY LEVELS: According to the U.S. Bureau of Labor Statistics, the annual median earnings for dentists are **$129,900**, with variations based on years in practice, location within the United States, hours worked, and specialty.

COLLEGE VS. REALITY

How would you compare the reality of your profession to the picture you had of it while in school?

The nature of dental school and its emphasis on clinical training the last two years gave me a good reality of the medical side of the practice.

—General dentistry, 6 years, Austin, Texas

There is a lot more to a successful dental practice than the academic preparation you receive in school. You also have to become an entrepreneur who is running a small business. There is much more to this side of the practice than I anticipated.

—**Maxillofacial surgeon, 3 years,**
Memphis, Tennessee

Based on the curriculum in dental school and the practical, hands-on clinical experience you receive, I felt I had a relatively good overview of a dentistry practice.

—**General dentistry, 9 years, Medina, Ohio**

. . .

How would you rate your collegiate and graduate courses in preparing you for your profession on a scale of 1 to 10, with 10 being the best?

The last two years of your four-year dental school training concentrate on clinical work and patient treatment, so as regards the medical aspects of being a dentist, every graduate should be generally well prepared.

—**General dentistry, 11 years,**
Salt Lake City, Utah

It can be a huge investment to start up a dental practice, and even if you do not hang out your own shingle but rather start as an associate in an existing

practice, ultimately you are going to be involved in a wide range of business- and employment-related issues. With that in mind, I wish I had taken a few more business courses along the way.

—**Orthodontist, 10 years,**
Springfield, Missouri

I do not know of a dental school that does not conduct its own clinical practice. If you want to be prepared in dentistry, the clinical experience is there to be had. Plus, you learn to relate with people whose socioeconomic level has not afforded them frequent interaction with dentists. I felt well prepared when I entered the real world.

—**Periodontist, 14 years,**
Providence, Rhode Island

THE BIGGEST SURPRISE

What most surprised you about your chosen profession?

The rapid advancement in materials, which has allowed general dentists to expand to some degree into orthodontic work without having to spend the additional years of training in that specialty.

—**General dentistry, 16 years,**
Portland, Oregon

How the obsession in this country with everything cosmetic has allowed dentists to create a patient environment that includes aspects that have less to do with dentistry and more to do with marketing.

—General dentistry, 22 years,
Albuquerque, New Mexico

How intensely competitive the profession is.

—General dentistry, 8 years,
Raleigh, North Carolina

HOURS AND ADVANCEMENT

How many hours do you work each week at your career?

It depends on how much emergency work I am asked to perform, but a normal week of consultations, follow-ups, surgical procedures, supervisory duties, dictating charts, and reviewing literature usually equates to about a fifty-five-hour workweek.

—Oral surgeon, 12 years,
Lexington, Kentucky

I have been able to build up my practice and have a sufficient mix of other dentists and support staff so that my workweek consists of three and a half days in the office seeing patients.

—General dentistry, 24 years,
Baltimore, Maryland

With an active patient roster of several thousand, I could work sixty hours a week if I chose to, but I limit work to

four days a week. For me it is a quality-of-life issue.

—General dentistry, 16 years,
Winter Park, Florida

. . .

Have you found advancement within your career easy or difficult?

"Advancement" is the wrong term. Success as a dentist is measured in the number of active clients, and that in turn comes to a large extent from referrals.

—Maxillofacial surgeon, 17 years,
Hartford, Connecticut

If you equate advancement with increased income, then I have found advancement relatively easy. As your practice grows, you can produce an excellent income.

—General dentistry, 14 years,
Richmond, Virginia

There will always be a need for dentists, and the variety of procedures that the general public now deem as the norm should create an environment for a sound dental practice to advance with a growing client base.

—General dentistry, 11 years,
Montclair, New Jersey

THE BEST AND THE WORST

What do you spend most of your day doing? Describe a typical day.

A typical day is made up of four to five checkups, six to seven consultations, four to five wisdom teeth removals, managing my staff of seven, and taking multiple phone calls relating to the medical and business side of my practice.

—**Maxillofacial surgeon, 9 years,**
Sandy Springs, Georgia

My days are patient driven. The setup of my practice and my staff allows me to see an average of twenty-five patients a day, for a combination of checkups and procedures.

—**General dentistry, 21 years,**
Florence, South Carolina

I work four days a week, and my exact daily activities are dictated by the particular needs of my patients. With a family practice, my staff and I perform a wide variety of general procedures. To maximize the efficiency of my practice, I try to keep all my rooms full as much as possible and have my dental assistants, technicians, and hygienists handle as much of the load as possible as pertains to cleanings, X-rays, patient instruction, and procedure preparation.

—**General dentistry, 13 years,**
Baton Rouge, Louisiana

. . .

What are the best parts of your profession?

I like the predictability of what I encounter on a daily basis. While I participated earlier in my career in more emergency procedures resulting from car accidents and other intense traumas, currently my practice is for the most part centered around the removal of wisdom teeth. I know what to expect with most patients, and I am comfortable in matching my skills to the situation so as to provide my patients with a good overall experience.

—**Oral surgeon, 8 years, Nashville, Tennessee**

The autonomy, the flexibility of hours, the financial rewards, and the satisfaction of assisting others achieve a more confident profile through an improved smile.

—**Orthodontist, 12 years, Tucson, Arizona**

The ability to make an excellent living and work less than forty hours per week.

—**General dentist, 17 years,**
Mobile, Alabama

. . .

What are the least enjoyable aspects of your profession?

If you choose to be a dentist, and have an interest in specializing, you can spend as much as six to nine years in school after college. If you do not come from a wealthy family and are taking out student loans, that can be an enormous debt with which you have to start your profession.

—**Maxillofacial surgeon, 9 years, Omaha, Nebraska**

There is a certain amount of repetition in the procedures that one follows as a dentist, but anyone who elected to become a general dentist knew that going into the profession.

—**General dentistry, 15 years, Troy, Michigan**

As an oral surgeon there can be high levels of stress that are associated with the precision and skill needed in the anesthesiology aspects of oral surgery.

—**Oral surgeon, 6 years, Plano, Texas**

CHANGES IN THE PROFESSION

What changes do you foresee for your profession?

Materials, along with procedures, will continue to improve, opening up more avenues for general dentists for treatments that were exclusively the province of oral surgeons or other specialists.

—**General dentistry, 16 years, Aiken, South Carolina**

The science of dentistry in the next decade has the potential to expand significantly in such areas as protein profiling, saliva-based diagnostic testing for oral cancer, more research linking oral health with systemic health, improved computer imagery, expanded laser technology, lab-on-a-chip diagnostic tools, new restorative procedures, bio-adhesives, better composites, and molecular-based screening.

—**Dental educator, 22 years, Dallas, Texas**

A potential shortage of general dentists nationwide as more and more practitioners retire at the same time as dental school graduates elect to pursue postgraduate programs to prepare for a dental specialty.

—**Public health dentist, 18 years, Phoenix, Arizona**

WOULD YOU DO IT ALL OVER AGAIN?

Do you find your daily job fulfilling?

Yes. It has allowed me to be an entrepreneur and a health-care professional at the same time while making an excellent living with very manageable hours.

—**General dentistry, 23 years, Pittsburgh, Pennsylvania**

Dentistry is an excellent way to help others, generate a nice income, be part of your community, and not have the stress and hours of a physician.

—**Pediatric dentistry, 17 years, Roswell, Georgia**

Initially, I enjoyed my practice, but after ten years I started to become bored from the lack of academic challenge and the repetition of procedures.

—**General dentistry, 12 years,
Colorado Springs, Colorado**

. . .

Would you choose the same profession again?

Dental surgery matches well with my interests and my skills. I am a perfectionist who loves working with my hands. I am confident in my abilities and in the results that I know I can produce for my patients.

—**Maxillofacial surgeon, 10 years,
Wilmington, Delaware**

No. I would go into anesthesiology. There is an art to this aspect of my profession, and I think I would have enjoyed concentrating on this specialty of medicine more than on the dental side of my practice, and at the same time I could have made more money while investing less capital initially.

—**Oral surgeon, 14 years,
Altamonte Springs, Florida**

Yes. Dentistry has allowed me to participate in the world of medicine, improve people's health and appearance, and provide for my family at a very comfortable level, and not have to work sixty to seventy hours a week.

—**Orthodonist, 16 years, Lexington, Kentucky**

SO YOU WANT TO BE A
VETERINARIAN

Veterinary medicine is a broad discipline that offers many career choices, including general practice, specialty practice, food animal medicine, research, and academic positions. I feel that most DVMs [doctors of veterinarian medicine] could find a niche for themselves even as their needs or interests change. I have recently changed the focus of my practice to Chinese medicine and acupuncture, using this as an adjunct to Western, or "allopathic," medicine to improve my patients' quality of life. The fact that after ten years in general practice I could learn a new skill — acupuncture — and then create my own business offering this skill to those who need it is a good example of the flexibility of this career choice.

There are more pets in the United States than there are people, which means that veterinarians have more potential clients than do doctors. The word "pet" has been part of the English language since the 1600s, and the first school of veterinary medicine opened in France in 1762. Beginning in the 1800s people increasingly viewed animals, especially dogs, as companions and not just workers. Today, most Americans consider their pets members of their family, and studies indicate that pets have a positive impact on overall human happiness. According to the American Pet Products Manufacturers Association (APPMA), in 2006 Americans spent an estimated $38.4 billion on food, veterinary care, and supplies for their pets. This was a 35 percent increase from the $28.5 billion spent in 2001.

The profession of veterinary medicine has expanded as well. Today veterinarians diagnose and treat sick and injured animals using a broad array of instruments and techniques, from traditional medical instruments like stethoscopes, thermometers, and X-rays to sophisticated and state-of-the-art equipment and procedures like electron microscopes, laser surgery, radiation therapy, and ultrasound. Even the use of acupuncture on pets is now becoming accepted in the United States. Pet owners are taking advantage of this advanced medical care, and as a consequence they are spending ever-larger sums on the care of their animals.

A *veterinarian*, or *doctor of veterinarian medicine*, diagnoses animal disease, treats sick and injured animals using medicine and surgery, and advises owners of proper care for their animals. Yet the world of veterinary medicine offers many more opportunities than simply taking care of pets or livestock. Pharmaceutical and biomedical research firms hire veterinarians to develop, test, and supervise the production of drugs, chemicals, and various biological products. Veterinarians play key roles in the research of antibiotics and vaccines, both those designed for animals and those made for human use. Also, veterinarians play a critical role in public health by assuring a safe food supply and in limiting the spread of disease.

In America, with a growing population and a more involved degree of pet care, demand for veterinarians is expected to remain high for the future. In fact the U.S. Department of Labor names veterinary medicine as one of the fastest-growing occupations, with large increases in employment anticipated through at least 2014. Yet becoming a veterinarian is not easy. Due to the limited number of accredited schools of veterinary medicine in the United States, competition is keen. An aptitude for and interest in biological sciences are important, along with an inquiring mind and keen powers of observation. As in all the health professions, communication skills are vital. Veterinarians must deal effectively with pet owners, not just their animals, particularly during difficult times, such as when euthanizing animals.

Approximately 70 percent of veterinarians are owners or employees of established veterinary practices, with half of these exclusively treating small or companion animals. Dogs and cats represent the highest number of companion animals, but these also include birds, reptiles, and rabbits. A smaller number of established practices deal exclusively with large animals such as horses and cows. Outside private practice, opportunities in veterinary medicine abound. Within the government sector, employment is offered by the U.S. Department of Agriculture, Health and Human Services, and even the Department of Homeland Security (to help deal with the threat of terrorism through a contaminated food supply). Pharmaceutical and biomedical firms offer positions for those who prefer research, and zoos, aquariums, nature centers, and firms that provide laboratory animals offer opportunities for those with degrees in veterinary medicine.

As the level of medical care for animals increases, more veterinarians are electing to specialize in areas like surgery, cardiology, internal medicine, ophthalmology, radiology, neurology, oncology, critical care/emergency, and dentistry. While the level and sophistication of care for animals continue to expand and evolve, the income earned by veterinarians continues to lag behind that of their counterparts in the medical world.

BY THE NUMBERS

EMPLOYMENT LEVELS: According to the U.S. Bureau of Labor Statistics, veterinarians hold 61,000 jobs in the United States.

ACADEMIC REQUIREMENTS: Prospective veterinarians must graduate with a degree in veterinarian medicine (DVM) from a four-year program at an accredited college of veterinarian medicine. They then must pass the National Board of Veterinarian Medicine exam before they can obtain a license; separate licenses are issued by each state. There are twenty-eight veterinarian colleges in the United States.

AVERAGE SALARY LEVELS: According to the American Veterinary Medical Association, average starting salaries vary depending on the type of practice, but they range from **$38,600** to **$50,870**. The U.S. Bureau of Labor Statistics indicates that the median annual earnings for veterinarians is **$66,590**.

COLLEGE VS. REALITY

How would you compare the reality of your profession to the picture you had of it while in school?

I had worked in veterinary clinics during school, so I knew what the real-world environment of veterinary medicine was generally like. What I did not fully appreciate were the long hours necessary to build a successful practice.

—Small-animal veterinarian, 4 years,
Winston Salem, North Carolina

In veterinary school you are so focused on the animals and the treatments that you forget that with every pet there comes an owner or two. The injection of the human element changes everything, and from my perspective not always for the better.

—Mixed-practice veterinarian, 3 years,
Jackson, Tennessee

I was naïve in my pre-practice appreciation of the day-to-day world of a veterinarian. It is a much more stressful job than I imagined. I did not realize how large a factor human emotions would play in my daily practice.

—Small-animal veterinarian, 6 years,
Spartanburg, South Carolina

. . .

How would you rate your collegiate and graduate courses in preparing you for your profession on a scale of 1 to 10, with 10 being the best?

My veterinary school courses were excellent in preparing me for the medical side. I wish there had been more courses relating to the business side of the practice.

—Large-animal veterinarian, 5 years,
Lawton, Oklahoma

As a student I focused on learning as much about medical techniques as possible. But the reality is, until you are in a practice setting, you don't fully appreciate what all is encompassed in being an effective practitioner.

—Equine veterinarian, 7 years, Ocala, Florida

I would give my undergraduate courses an 8 and my graduate courses and training a 9. I would also encourage anyone who wishes to make this a career to work part-time in a veterinarian office while an undergraduate. It will help you determine if you are heading on the right career path.

—Small-animal veterinarian, 11 years, Roanoke, Virginia

THE BIGGEST SURPRISE

What most surprised you about your chosen profession?

The long hours and low pay compared to those in other professions for which you must complete this much education.

—Small-animal veterinarian, 4 years, Jackson, Mississippi

How much the practice of veterinary medicine is centered around people rather than animals. If you are not a people person, and not one who can patiently handle people and their concerns and often their emotions, you should reconsider being a vet.

—General-practice veterinarian, 21 years, Charlotte, North Carolina

The group politics of the profession on a regional and national basis, and how that can affect one's career opportunities as relates to placement in certain specialty programs.

—Cardiology specialist, 9 years, Tampa, Florida

HOURS AND ADVANCEMENT

How many hours do you work each week at your career?

Fifty to sixty.

—Mixed-practice veterinarian, 18 years, Cheyenne, Wyoming

Forty-five to fifty-five.

—Small-animal veterinarian, 8 years, New Haven, Connecticut

Fifty to sixty.

—Veterinarian surgeon, 14 years, Knoxville, Tennessee

. . .

Have you found advancement within your career easy or difficult?

Unless you pursue food animal medicine, research, or academia, veterinarian medicine does not really compare to other professions. You either work for another vet or you are a partner/owner.

—Small-animal veterinarian, 15 years, Salem, Oregon

Women's salaries are still not on par with men's salaries, but I think that is gradually changing as now more women than men are entering the profession.

> —Oncology specialist, 11 years,
> Atlanta, Georgia

A lot of that depends on which particular group you associate yourself with. Some are more geared to encouraging partnership status. Veterinary practices are popping up around the country that only employ specialists, each with their own discipline, and this business structure promotes a more equitable income arrangement.

> —Internal medicine specialist, 15 years,
> San Diego, California

THE BEST AND THE WORST

What do you spend most of your day doing? Describe a typical day.

Most days consist of a mix of reviewing charts for the day, performing procedures, taking appointments, listening to pet owners, and updating chart notes.

> —Small-animal veterinarian, 9 years,
> Frankfort, Kentucky

My week is usually divided into appointments one day and performing surgeries the next. Of course, I am also responding to calls from other veterinarians about referrals to our office.

> —Veterinarian surgeon, 14 years,
> Ann Arbor, Michigan

My days are filled with inspections of various animal-raising operations, meat-producing plants, and related facilities. With an enhanced focus on food safety and disease control as a result of the broad response to terror attacks, this type of activity by veterinarians will only need to increase in the United States.

> —Government veterinarian, 7 years,
> Fayetteville, Arkansas

. . .

What are the best parts of your profession?

The long-term relationships I have made with my clients and their pets.

> —Small-animal veterinarian, 18 years,
> Elmhurst, Illinois

The evolution of veterinary medicine and the opportunity to improve our service to our patients and their owners.

> —General-practice veterinarian, 24 years,
> Dayton, Ohio

Improving the quality of life for my patients.

> —Small-animal veterinarian, 10 years,
> Topeka, Kansas

. . .

What are the least enjoyable aspects of your profession?

Euthanizing pets. No matter how many times it is the right thing to do, it is tough. People are very, very attached to their pets.

—Small-animal veterinarian, 7 years,
Huntington, West Virginia

The least enjoyable aspect is trying to make clients understand the cost of doing business, especially for the advanced procedures we are performing. Our level of care is very similar to that in the human field in many ways, yet some clients fail to grasp the value we provide.

—Veterinarian surgeon, 12 years,
Fort Worth, Texas

The low pay for the hours you put in to be an effective and responsive veterinarian.

—Small-animal veterinarian, 6 years,
Columbia, South Carolina

CHANGES IN THE PROFESSION

What changes do you foresee for your profession?

More women entering the profession and a resultant change to more flexible working hours to accommodate family responsibilities.

—Small-animal veterinarian, 9 years,
Parkville, Maryland

An increase in specialties and an advanced level of medical procedures and expertise available for patient treatment.

—Orthopedic specialist, 15 years,
Indianapolis, Indiana

A gradual move to an overall veterinarian practice which patterns itself more and more after medical practice on humans, including a willingness to expand insurance coverage for procedures and to embrace new trends, such as medical ideas from other parts of the world, like holistic medicine.

—General-practice veterinarian, 5 years,
Norcross, Georgia

WOULD YOU DO IT ALL OVER AGAIN?

Do you find your daily job fulfilling?

I enjoy practicing medicine because it is so challenging and interesting. But the stress level is so high — dealing with sick animals, putting to sleep animals whom I believe I can help but whose owners are unwilling to try, trying to figure out very challenging cases. Am I doing all I can to increase the quality of life of every patient I see, from the healthy puppy down to the very old and ill cat? I want to help people, but ultimately I am an advocate of the pet, the voice it doesn't have.

—Small-animal veterinarian, 2 years,
St. Louis, Missouri

Yes. I am helping people with their pets, who for many people are members of their family for whom they want the best.

—Small-animal veterinarian, 16 years,
Greenville, South Carolina

My days are varied, which I like. And the profession is broadening its overall approach to treatment, which I see as a long-term plus. But the hours are long and the pay is low on a comparative basis.

—General-practice veterinarian, 6 years,
New Bern, North Carolina

. . .

Would you choose the same profession again?

Absolutely. It is a profession that is now quickly evolving after many decades of remaining tied to its old roots. I want to participate in those improvements, including better medical options for owners and their animals.

—Veterinarian surgeon, 8 years,
Providence, Rhode Island

I think I would. Veterinary medicine is a broad discipline that offers many career choices, including general practice, specialty practice, food animal medicine, research, and academic positions. I feel that most DVMs [doctors of veterinarian medicine] could find a niche for themselves even as their needs or interests change. I have recently changed the focus of my practice to Chinese medicine and acupuncture, using this as an adjunct to Western, or "allopathic," medicine to improve my patients' quality of life. The fact that after ten years in general practice I could learn a new skill — acupuncture — and then create my own business offering this skill to those who need it is a good example of the flexibility of this career choice.

—Holistic specialist, 12 years,
Madison, Wisconsin

No. Based upon the low income level compared to medical practices for people, if I had to do it all over again, I would have followed my love for medicine into a career of caring for humans.

—Small-animal veterinarian, 7 years,
Scranton, Pennsylvania

CAREERS IN

Architecture and Engineering

SO YOU WANT TO BE AN ARCHITECT

The profession can be very frustrating in that you have to deal with so many different consultants — civil engineers, landscape architects, structural engineers, mechanical engineers, plumbing engineers, electrical engineers, lighting designers, interior designers, surveyors, geotechnical engineers, acoustical consultants, and so on — at one time and on one project. But aside from the consultants there is the challenge to meet the sometimes demanding goals of the owner. Then there is the contractor [moment of silence]...the construction phase is probably the most intense part of the project.

People need places in which to live, work, learn, meet, manufacture, govern, shop, and eat. All these buildings and spaces must be designed, and that is where architects come in. Trained in the art and science of building design, architects blend creativity with function by transforming these human needs into spatial concepts, and then those concepts into images and plans.

In function, if not in name, architects have existed ever since cavemen left their caves and built the first huts. It was the Romans who developed concrete vaulting, which allowed for permanent masonry buildings, and since the Industrial Revolution, iron and steel have been core building materials. With computers and new manufacturing techniques today, architects have never had so many options at their disposal.

An architect's job requires knowledge of a wide range of fields. Architects are expected to know construction methods, engineering principles and practices, material characteristics, construction costs, and computer-aided design and drafting (CADD) technology. The ability to both conceptualize and communicate is essential. Great design ideas may never become actual buildings without the ability to effectively communicate with those who will be using and paying for the structures.

It is generally helpful to have artistic skills and drawing ability, and to be good at math and have an understanding of spatial relationships, but it is just as important to be able to coordinate information, manage and supervise others, work well with both clients and contractors, and be flexible, since building plans often need to be revised as needs and budgets change. Most architects work within the framework of a design or project team, which usually consists of *designers*, who specialize in design development; *structural designers*, who design the frame of the structure under the direction of the architect; a *project manager* or *superintendent*, who ensures that the detail drawings are completed as directed by the architect; and a *specification writer* or *estimator*, who produces a project manual itemizing the materials to be used in construction and their method of installation.

In broad strokes, the outlook for architectural jobs is encouraging. There will always be a need for housing, industrial plants, office buildings, shopping centers, airports, schools, and so on, particularly as the world population grows. And as people continue to live longer, there will be more demand for health-care and retirement facilities.

Yet there are some clouds on the horizon. In the past decade, some architectural firms have begun outsourcing to other countries, such as India and China, for the drafting of construction documents for large-scale commercial and residential projects. This trend is expected to continue, and it will have a negative impact on employment growth, especially for lower-level architects and interns. In fact, the number of independent architects in the United States has been flat, if not declining, in the past few years. To maximize business opportunities, many architects specialize by focusing on only one type of project, such as schools, hospitals, or residential structures.

Architects maintain a unique position within society. In addition to designing practical, functional buildings, architects must also be sure that the structures they design are safe and conform to all applicable codes, laws, and regulations. But also, the profession as a whole focuses on improving our society's overall quality of life by building healthy, sustainable, safe, and livable communities. A blend of creativity and function, architecture is an expression of the individual maker and of the society the maker lives in; architecture evolves with human civilization, and through their buildings architects create a legacy that reflects the culture of each generation.

BY THE NUMBERS

EMPLOYMENT LEVELS: According to the U.S. Bureau of Labor Statistics, there are 129,000 licensed architects employed in the United States.

ACADEMIC REQUIREMENTS: To become a practicing architect, you must earn a professional degree in architecture. Most programs take five years to complete, after which graduates must participate in an Intern Development Program by working under the supervision of a licensed architect. In most states, intern programs last three years, although in a few states they are longer. Once you have completed the Intern Development Program, you are permitted to take the Architect Registration Examination (ARE); you must pass all the divisions of the ARE before you can become licensed. All fifty states and the District of Columbia require architects to be licensed.

AVERAGE SALARY LEVELS: According to the U.S. Bureau of Labor Statistics, the median annual salary for architects is **$60,300**; overall, salaries range from around **$38,060** to **$99,800** and up.

COLLEGE VS. REALITY

How would you compare the reality of your profession to the picture you had of it while in school?

The picture I had of architecture and the reality of day-to-day architecture are broadly different. I anticipated much more of an artistic and creative design environment, rather than one dominated by construction details and change orders.

—Architect, 8 years, Milwaukee, Wisconsin

I had the Frank Lloyd Wright image of the architect being the genius behind the project — the one looked up to by everyone involved. In reality, the architect is just another person an owner employs to complete a project, along with the contractor, the engineer, the attorney, and the accountant. The idea of translating one's architectural vision to the project is a rarity when one is designing schools, government buildings, and nursing homes.

—Architect, 10 years, Charlotte, North Carolina

The practice of architecture is much more about constructions details and being part of a team than I ever anticipated. Projects can take six months of preconstruction work and a year or more in construction. My idea of creating a great design and then moving on to the next one was far from reality. As the saying goes, "The devil is in the details."

—Architect, 6 years, Alpharetta, Georgia

. . .

How would you rate your collegiate and graduate courses in preparing you for your profession on a scale of 1 to 10, with 10 being the best?

On design it was a 9. But design represents only a fraction of the daily life of an architect. What was missing were courses that supported the construction side of projects, which take up much more time than the design side.

—Architect, 11 years, Hoover, Alabama

A 6. My college and graduate courses concentrated on design. What were lacking were the courses on the business side of the profession.

—Architect, 5 years, Tucson, Arizona

I would give it a 10 on design and a 2 on the business reality of being an architect. I was not provided enough information about construction administration, dealing with contractors, finance, government approvals, and securing business.

—Architect, 12 years, Tampa, Florida

THE BIGGEST SURPRISE

What most surprised you about your chosen profession?

The comparatively low pay for the amount of education required and the daily stress of meeting deadlines.

—Architect, 7 years, Grand Rapids, Michigan

The repetitive nature of so much of the work. If you are doing commercial work, the repetition in details and specifications gets to you after several years. The artistic side of architecture that attracted me often seems like a distant memory.

—Architect, 14 years, Boulder, Colorado

The lack of individuality. Artistic people usually observe from the outside and then see how to best translate what they observe in a design or an interpretation. In architecture, you are constantly thrown into a team environment by the mere nature of construction, and it becomes more of a job and less of an expression of design.

—Architect, 9 years, Framingham, Massachusetts

HOURS AND ADVANCEMENT

How many hours do you work each week at your career?

Fifty.

—Architect, 14 years, Louisville, Kentucky

Fifty-five to sixty.

—Architect, 6 years, Memphis, Tennessee

Fifty to sixty.

—Architect, 13 years, Seattle, Washington

. . .

Have you found advancement within your career easy or difficult?

Easy at first, but I have hit a ceiling. I still seem to be viewed as the new kid on the block by my bosses, as I was five years ago.

—Architect, 8 years, Arlington, Virginia

It depends on the proper blend of expertise that you acquire in one particular aspect of architecture. If you can specialize in one aspect, and be very good at it, the business will come, and with it the advancement, or if not, the opportunity to start your own firm.

—Architect, 15 years, Irving, Texas

Architecture is a career, not a job. You advance in this career at your own pace. Architecture can be thought of like a diamond; there are many facets to this career. You choose the facet you want to be involved in.

—Architect, 31 years, Nashville, Tennessee

THE BEST AND THE WORST

What do you spend most of your day doing? Describe a typical day.

A good day consists of a proper balance between working on new designs and moving ahead on existing projects.

—Architect, 22 years, Wilmington, Delaware

Most days are a mixture of different tasks on multiple projects and can include such things as working with a design team on a new project, meeting on-site with contractors and subcontractors,

updating owners, and responding to the endless emails.

—Architect, 7 years, New Rochelle, New York

Most days are different but are usually made up in large part of replying to questions from contractors, engineers, or owners. As an architect you have to learn the art of keeping all your current projects moving on schedule and on budget, meeting deadlines, and sometime in between, securing new business.

—Architect, 19 years, Austin, Texas

. . .

What are the best parts of your profession?

The design aspects of the project. It is why I became an architect.

—Architect, 12 years,
Baton Rouge, Louisiana

The completion of a project — finally seeing years of work come together.

—Architect, 12 years,
Sacramento, California

Improving the enjoyment of life for many people through the design of buildings that will impact people's lives for decades.

—Architect, 16 years, Salt Lake City, Utah

. . .

What are the least enjoyable aspects of your profession?

The stress of meeting deadlines and the low pay you receive for meeting those deadlines.

—Architect, 7 years,
Overland Park, Kansas

The way the process works, a set of drawings and specifications is always missing something. And the architect is ultimately responsible since all engineers work for us. Both the architect and the contractor are contracted with the owner. When a mistake or omission comes up, it adds costs to the project. A contentious or aggressive contractor can unduly influence the owner and make the architect look bad.

—Architect, 20 years, Atlanta, Georgia

The profession can be very frustrating in that you have to deal with so many different consultants — civil engineers, landscape architects, structural engineers, mechanical engineers, plumbing engineers, electrical engineers, lighting designers, interior designers, surveyors, geotechnical engineers, acoustical consultants, and so on — at one time and on one project. But aside from the consultants there is the challenge to meet the sometimes demanding goals of the owner. Then there is the *contractor* [moment of silence]...the construction

phase is probably the most intense part of the project.

—Architect, 8 years, Antioch, Tennessee

CHANGES IN THE PROFESSION

What changes do you foresee for your profession?

Fewer people going into architecture because of the better income potential in professions that are less detailed and stressful.

—Architect, 15 years, Detroit, Michigan

More computer-driven work, and the offshoring of more and more construction documents to countries like India.

—Architect, 10 years, Savannah, Georgia

Moving away from the connection between art and architecture and from the traditional ability to draw one's designs.

—Architect, 14 years, Spartanburg, South Carolina

WOULD YOU DO IT ALL OVER AGAIN?

Do you find your daily job fulfilling?

I like some aspects of my career as an architect, such as design work, but I dislike the retentive nature of other aspects, such as construction administration, and the political aspects of getting approvals and securing public projects.

—**Architect, 9 years, Phoenix, Arizona**

When you enter architecture you have to enter the profession for the love of it. If you are looking for recognition, it may come but you have to have infinite patience. Most architects do not make a real name for themselves until they have practiced for several decades. You have to love the work for the work's sake.

—**Architect, 24 years, Ft. Lauderdale, Florida**

No. You are underpaid for the significance of the work you perform and the responsibility you are given.

—**Architect, 7 years, Kansas City, Kansas**

. . .

Would you choose the same profession again?

Yes. Architecture is the perfect blend of creativity and mastering technical challenges.

—**Architect, 24 years, Cleveland, Ohio**

Absolutely NOT! This is a thankless career with long hours, high stress, and low pay. I would definitely do something where I made my own hours and actually spent time with my family.

—**Architect, 6 years, Nashville, Tennessee**

I love architecture but hate being at the mercy of developers, so I would choose rather to teach architecture so that my love for design could be pursued, but on a more predictable schedule.

—**Architect, 13 years, Philadelphia, Pennsylvania**

SO YOU WANT TO BE AN ENGINEER

There are a variety of different jobs in the profession, many of which require a larger range of business skills than are currently taught in engineering school. The surprising thing to me when I began my career was how the job changes as you advance. There is no method for career advancement as purely a designer. All advancement requires accepting supervisory and management responsibilities.

Who figured out how to get running water from a mountain stream to the baths and kitchens of a city? Who developed new ways to travel by wheel and boat across continents and oceans? Who figured out how humans could communicate with one another in an instant from opposite sides of the world? Who unlocked the secrets for building the Egyptian pyramids, the first airplane at Kitty Hawk, and the Apollo rockets that allowed Neil Armstrong to walk on the moon? These marvels were the results of the creative and analytical minds of the people we call engineers.

Engineering is the application of the physical sciences and mathematics to construct engines, machines, conveyances, and complex products;

engineers solve humankind's technical problems — how we can get from point A to point B and what we need, and so on — and they develop techniques that hopefully solve these problems in the most economical ways. There are five general areas in which engineers are involved on a daily basis: *design*, *development*, *testing*, *production*, and *maintenance*. Even more than most professions, specialization is the norm. The Standard Occupational Classification system recognizes seventeen different specialties within the profession of engineering: *aerospace engineers*, *agricultural engineers*, *biomedical engineers*, *chemical engineers*, *civil engineers*, *computer engineers*, *electrical engineers*, *electronic engineers*, *environmental engineers*, *health and safety engineers*, *industrial engineers*, *marine engineers*, *materials engineers*, *mechanical engineers*, *mining and geological engineers*, *nuclear engineers*, and *petroleum engineers*.

This chapter can't cover all these engineering specialties, but it provides insights from engineers who design bridges, tunnels, and water supply, and sewage systems (*civil engineers*); who design and test new products (*materials engineers*); who monitor water quality and are involved in other public health issues (*environmental engineers*); and more. I have elected to include a few observations in this chapter from engineers in the field of information technology since they are part of the broad field of engineering. However, in light of the integral nature that information technology has taken on in our everyday lives, I have also included a separate chapter (on page 149) on computer engineers, both hardware and software.

Most of us take engineers for granted in our daily lives. We just assume that when we turn on the faucet, water will be there; that when we start our cars, the engine will fire up, and our local gas station will have fuel; that when we drive, the highways and bridges won't crumble; and that when we want to talk to someone, our cell phones will reach them. Yet the world of computers has finally bestowed upon engineers a measure of public recognition and even, occasionally, of cool. Though still often referred to as "geeks" (such as on the Geek Squad commercials on television), engineers begin to feel the love when they become culture-shaping billionaires (like Bill Gates, cofounder of Microsoft, and Larry Page and Sergey Brin, cofounders of Google).

The need for engineers is likely to remain constant as our world evolves and changes. Global issues require bright minds that can apply mathematics and the physical sciences to solve complex problems. For instance, as fossil fuels become more scarce worldwide, the global population (and its need for energy) keeps growing. Alternative fuel sources will be required; in addition, over 20 percent of the world's population still does not have access to reliable potable water. Global climatic changes may require new agricultural methods. Plus, as technology evolves at lightning speed, every field will be looking for new, cheaper solutions to old problems.

And who will be the ones who keep up with all the technological changes and who find solutions to the world's problems?

Engineers.

BY THE NUMBERS

EMPLOYMENT LEVELS: According to the U.S. Bureau of Labor Statistics, there are over 1.4 million engineers in the United States. Of this, there are approximately 550,000 engineering jobs in manufacturing; approximately 370,000 engineers work in the professional, scientific, and technical services sector; and the remainder of engineers are either self-employed or working for the government at the local, state, or federal level.

ACADEMIC REQUIREMENTS: To get an entry-level engineering job, all you need is a four-year undergraduate degree (usually a Bachelor of Engineering, but sometimes a Bachelor of Science). To become a Professional Engineer (or PE), you need to be licensed and have at least four years of relevant work experience (required by all fifty states and the District of Columbia).

AVERAGE SALARY LEVELS: Salary levels differ greatly by specialty. For example, agricultural engineers have a median starting salary of **$43,270**, while petroleum engineers have a median starting salary of **$65,350**.

COLLEGE VS. REALITY

How would you compare the reality of your profession to the picture you had of it while in school?

While my college courses do not mesh with what I do every day, they did teach me the necessary theories of how things function, which is fundamental to everything that is engineering.

—Materials engineer, 15 years,
Denver, Colorado

While my engineering courses were excellent for teaching analytical thinking and problem solving, I wish there had been some general business skills taught as well.

—Civil engineer, 9 years,
Milwaukee, Wisconsin

My job is much more boring and more behind a desk than what I imagined. I thought I would be working in the field more — taking samples and whatnot.

—Environmental engineer, 8 years,
Allentown, Pennsylvania

. . .

How would you rate your collegiate and graduate courses in preparing you for your profession on a scale of 1 to 10, with 10 being the best?

5. My collegiate career was less effective in preparing me, but only because I didn't take advantage of opportunities. Co-op is an option that shows you what you will be doing in "real life," but I didn't want to leave campus. You have to be focused enough to want more than a job and know what career you want.

—Mechanical engineer/operations
management, 5 years, Hermitage, Tennessee

My bachelor degree in engineering science and mechanics gets a 6. Most of the work I do is not based upon the coursework I studied in school. However, an engineering degree is a prerequisite for getting most product development positions. Without my degree I wouldn't have gotten any of the jobs I have held.

—Engineer, product development, 9 years, Sellersville, Pennsylvania

Reality is never as great as you picture it. However, I would give my college courses a 6 for at least establishing the parameters of what steps one must take as an engineer when analyzing and solving a technical issue.

—Chemical engineer, 15 years, Sacramento, California

THE BIGGEST SURPRISE

What most surprised you about your chosen profession?

The huge amount of paperwork involved when testing products.

—Materials engineer, 6 years, Newark, New Jersey

The very slow pace of approvals when working with governmental agencies.

—Environmental engineer, 7 years, St. Louis, Missouri

What surprised me the most is how the government has chosen to give financial incentives to corporations to outsource technical jobs. Before 2000, my career was on an excellent path, but now it has become much harder to find work.

—Computer software engineer, 20 years, Orlando, Florida

HOURS AND ADVANCEMENT

How many hours do you work each week at your career?

Forty hours or so in the office now that I have my PE license. Before that I also spent a lot of time studying for my exams in addition to fulfilling my full-time job obligations.

—Civil engineer, 8 years, Little Rock, Arkansas

Forty to fifty hours a week.

—Chemical engineer, 18 years, Atlanta, Georgia

Forty to forty-two hours is a standard week.

—Mechanical engineer, 21 years, Detroit, Michigan

. . .

Have you found advancement within your career easy or difficult?

It depends on what region of the country you work in, and what type of engineering you practice. If growth is booming, and you work with developers and construction, advancement will come relatively easily.

—Civil engineer, 10 years,
Irvine, California

In the past five years, it has become much more difficult.

—Software engineer, 17 years,
Philadelphia, Pennsylvania

There are a variety of different jobs in the profession, many of which require a larger range of business skills than are currently taught in engineering school. The surprising thing to me when I began my career was how the job changes as you advance. There is no method for career advancement as purely a designer. All advancement requires accepting supervisory and management responsibilities.

—Civil engineer, 9 years,
Nashville, Tennessee

THE BEST AND THE WORST

What do you spend most of your day doing? Describe a typical day.

My usual day is a combination of sending and reviewing emails, updating design drawings, conferring with fellow engineers in the office who are handling other aspects of the same projects, and talking to clients.

—Civil engineer, 12 years,
Charleston, South Carolina

My typical day consists of either product development or testing. There is a lot of paperwork involved in documenting all the results of testing.

—Product design engineer, 18 years,
Kansas City, Kansas

Reviewing plans, discussing modifications with my supervisors, on-site inspections of projects, and meeting with contractors.

—Bridge design engineer, State Department
of Transportation, 6 years,
Springfield, Illinois

. . .

What are the best parts of your profession?

Seeing a project come to completion, and knowing you had a large part in it.

—Civil engineer, 10 years,
Charlotte, North Carolina

The intellectual challenge in solving technical problems.

—Computer engineer, 15 years,
Las Vegas, Nevada

Seeing a new product perform as it was designed to.

—Product design engineer, 22 years,
Cleveland, Ohio

. . .

What are the least enjoyable aspects of your profession?

The repetition in assignment. I take pride in my design work, but after fifty subdivisions, water runoff and storm drainage do not hold my interest like they once did.

—Civil engineer, 12 years,
Louisville, Kentucky

The lack of opportunities in what once was a booming profession.

—Computer engineer, 14 years,
Hartford, Connecticut

The lack of respect that engineers now receive compared to in the past. In the rush to build and develop everything possible, which dominated so much of the 1990s, engineers were bypassed in many instances in favor of contractors who professed skills and a level of competence beyond their degree of knowledge.

—Civil engineer, 22 years,
McLean, Virginia

CHANGES IN THE PROFESSION

How has your profession changed the most in the past five years?

As more and more companies manufacture their products outside the United States, more and more engineering work is being outsourced as well.

—Materials engineer, 22 years, Dayton, Ohio

Many design projects are now jointly being handled with engineers in Asia.

—Product development engineer, 16 years,
Baltimore, Maryland

With the exception of petroleum engineering and areas still experiencing brisk real estate development, on a national basis most engineering opportunities have cooled down somewhat over the past five years.

—Civil engineer, 25 years, Topeka, Kansas

· · ·

What changes do you foresee for your profession?

More and more engineering jobs going overseas.

—Chemical engineer, 16 years,
Rochester, New York

The outsourcing of more jobs to India, Asia, and China.

—Aerospace engineer, 11 years,
Seattle, Washington

The opportunity for a new boom in engineering with the need for alternative fuels and with the growth of nanotechnology.

—Professor of engineering, 28 years,
New York City

WOULD YOU DO IT ALL OVER AGAIN?

Do you find your daily job fulfilling?

Yes, very. Each day is an opportunity to paint a masterpiece in code. Even if I'm the only one who appreciates it!

—Electronics engineer and scientist, 27 years, Malabar, Florida

It is fulfilling when you arrive at the finished product or project, but getting there can become rather tedious.

—Civil engineer, 17 years, Omaha, Nebraska

My daily job is fulfilling at various times. Some projects are not as enjoyable as others, and I spend more time now on management issues and less time on design.

—Mechanical engineer, 19 years, Indianapolis, Indiana

. . .

Would you choose the same profession again?

Yes. It suits my skills, and I have found it pays well.

—Petroleum engineer, 22 years, Houston, Texas

No. I would select a profession where the work could not be so easily outsourced outside the country.

—Computer software engineer, 14 years, Los Angeles, California

Yes, but I would take some business courses along the way as well.

—Industrial engineer, 16 years, Chicago, Illinois

SO YOU WANT TO BE A LANDSCAPE ARCHITECT

The profession of landscape architecture is really beginning to shine right now. With the increase of environmental hurdles and regulations with which to comply, the demand for landscape architects is growing. We are not experts in any particular field, but rather we know something about a lot of different professions — engineering, construction, development, and planning. This broad knowledge base positions us well to be the point persons on a wide variety of projects as they are presented to various governmental bodies and agencies.

What do the Garden at the Arboretum at Harvard University; the Tanghe River Park in Qinhuangdao City, China; the Washington Mutual Center Roof Garden in Seattle, Washington; the Mount Tabor Middle School Rain Garden in Portland, Oregon; the Glacier Club Golf Course in Durango, Colorado; and the Malinalco House in Malinalco, Mexico, have in common? They are all award-winning designs by landscape architects.

What do landscape architects really do? Most of us appreciate when buildings and homes in our communities are surrounded by inviting landscapes, but it can be hard to pinpoint what, exactly, makes them appealing. Designing a landscape is much more than simply selecting some pretty shrubs and plants. Landscape architects look at both how a public space is best used and how it makes people feel to be in it, and landscape architecture is the art and science of analysis, planning, design, management, preservation, and rehabilitation of the land. It can be viewed as a mediation between architecture, topography, climate, and cultural history.

Landscape architecture goes back as far as the Romans. In the United States, Frederick Law Olmsted is considered the father of American landscape architecture. A writer, engineer, and visionary, Olmsted became the driving force behind many of America's urban parks, including New York City's Central Park. He also designed the grounds surrounding the United States Capitol, as well as those of the Biltmore Estate in North Carolina.

To a great extent, landscape architecture in the United States still follows in Olmsted's artful footsteps, working with a palette of light, shadow, and the blending of differing textures. But landscape architecture has also expanded into a much more diverse profession. Landscape architects are involved in urban design, open-space planning, stormwater mitigation, ecological restoration, urban renewal, residential design, greenways, regional and community planning, and the creation of creative and educational displays of water, light, sculpture, plant materials, and postindustrial and recycled materials.

The American Society of Landscape Architects (ASLA) has been around since 1899 and has somewhat less than twenty thousand members. In comparison, the American Institute of Architecture, which was formed in 1857, has over seventy-seven thousand members. Yet the ranks of landscape architects are growing, and according to the ASLA, the opportunities for employment remain good. Indeed, many communities and cities have become focused on "greening" their centers and public spaces, and environmental concerns (and restrictions) require careful planning societywide.

To push for more environmentally conscious design and to optimize energy use, the nonprofit Green Building Council was founded. One council effort is its LEED (Leadership in Energy and Environmental Design) certification program, which awards the LEED designation to individual architects and others. Landscape architects are at the forefront of the LEED movement, which promotes a whole-building approach to sustainability. This certification recognizes performance in five major areas of human and environmental health: sustainable site development, water savings, energy efficiency, materials selection, and indoor environmental quality.

Unlike architects, who make the majority of their income from commercial and public projects, the majority of landscape architects are involved in the design, planning, and installation of residential projects, such as subdivisions, apartment and condominium complexes, and retirement communities.

What kind of person would be suited for a career in landscape architecture? Individuals with visualization skills and originality, yet who can use mathematics and science to anticipate and solve problems. An entrepreneurial spirit also helps, as one in four landscape architects in the United States is self-employed.

As a profession, landscape architecture physically shapes our everyday world in an effort to inject a measure of tranquility and beauty into our busy lives. Through the design of parks and other public places, landscape architects offer us a place to find rest and refreshment and to allow for communal interaction — what Frederick Law Olmsted referred to as a "community soul."

BY THE NUMBERS

EMPLOYMENT LEVELS: According to the U.S. Bureau of Labor Statistics, there are approximately 25,000 landscape architects in the United States, with over 25 percent being self-employed. Others work as salaried employees for landscape architecture firms, engineering firms, municipalities, and real estate development companies.

ACADEMIC REQUIREMENTS: To become a landscape architect, you must complete either a four-year or five-year bachelor's degree in landscape architecture (which is offered by fifty-nine U.S. colleges and universities). Many colleges also offer a three-year master's degree designed for students with a bachelor's degree in another discipline. Forty-seven states require that landscape architects be licensed to practice by passing the Landscape Architecture Registration Examination (LARE). Before taking the LARE, you must work under the supervision of a registered landscape architect for anywhere from one to four years, depending on the jurisdiction.

AVERAGE SALARY LEVELS: According to the U.S. Bureau of Labor Statistics, the median earnings for landscape architects are **$53,120**. The annual income range is **$32,390** to **$90,850**.

COLLEGE VS. REALITY

How would you compare the reality of your profession to the picture you had of it while in school?

I pictured a practice where I was out in the field working on projects much more than I am. I spend the majority of time in the office.

—Landscape architect, 4 years,
Brookfield, Wisconsin

When you are in college, you do not fully appreciate the stress levels that can be associated with project deadlines.

—Landscape architect, 3 years,
Chesapeake, Virginia

There is much more people interaction than I anticipated while in college. I had a rather naïve picture of spending most of my time on design work. Instead, I spend most of my time managing projects or managing other people.

**—Landscape architect, 8 years,
Birmingham, Alabama**

. . .

How would you rate your collegiate and graduate courses in preparing you for your profession on a scale of 1 to 10, with 10 being the best?

I majored in landscape architecture, and the courses were very structured and did a good job in preparing me for landscape architecture from a design standpoint.

**—Landscape architect, 2 years,
Aurora, Illinois**

Many of my professors were also practicing landscape architects, and so we had the opportunity in the studio-based portion of my education to work on actual projects.

**—Landscape architect, 5 years,
Frederick, Maryland**

From a design standpoint, my college courses were instructive. What was lacking was enough emphasis in the business side of the profession.

—Landscape architect, 7 years, Akron, Ohio

THE BIGGEST SURPRISE

What most surprised you about your chosen profession?

How much time I spend at the office versus in the field. One of the attractions for me in landscape architecture was the chance to be outside rather than trapped indoors in an office environment.

**—Landscape architect, 8 years,
Wilmington, Delaware**

How many people do not understand what landscape architects do.

**—Landscape architect, 2 years,
Tallahassee, Florida**

The necessary interaction with so many other professionals and nonprofessionals while working on a project. I had a vision of much more design and fewer meetings.

**—Landscape architect, 10 years,
Decatur, Georgia**

HOURS AND ADVANCEMENT

How many hours do you work each week at your career?

It depends on the deadlines I am facing. It can vary from forty-five to fifty-five or sixty.

**—Landscape architect, 14 years,
Greenville, South Carolina**

It depends on my schedule. If my week includes making an appearance on behalf of a client before a governmental regulatory body, such as a planning commission, forty-five to fifty can easily stretch into fifty to fifty-five.

—Landscape architect, 19 years,
Paterson, New Jersey

Forty-five to fifty hours.

—Landscape architect, 9 years,
Grand Rapids, Michigan

. . .

Have you found advancement within your career easy or difficult?

There is a growing need for landscape architects. So if you get your work completed in a professional and timely manner, you can advance within your firm relatively quickly because there is more and more work out there.

—Landscape architect, 15 years,
Charlotte, North Carolina

It depends where you are employed. If you are in a small landscape architecture and design firm, the only way to truly advance after a few years is to become a partner on some basis. If you work for a large diversified engineering firm, advancement means less design work and more project management. Whether that equates with advancement is one's own individual assessment.

—Landscape architect, 7 years,
Springfield, Massachusetts

The profession of landscape architecture is currently experiencing a real burst of energy in virtually all areas of the country as environmental concerns and regulatory issues cause developers to seek the advice of landscape architects with more regularity.

—Landscape architect, 12 years,
Pittsburgh, Pennsylvania

THE BEST AND THE WORST

What do you spend most of your day doing? Describe a typical day.

My days are spent managing a variety of projects at various stages. I may have to devote some time to as many as a dozen different projects.

—Landscape architect, 17 years,
Atlanta, Georgia

I am in my second year, so I spend most of the day doing design work as it is assigned to me by my superiors.

—Landscape architect, 2 years,
Richmond, Virginia

My day could consist of any or all of the following: meeting with the landscape architects who work under me; meeting with clients to discuss a new project they wish to initiate; doing an initial design layout in broad strokes for a project and then passing it along to others in my division for more detailed design; signing off on preliminary and final plats for presentation to a governmental agency for approval; meetings with engineers in our firm to coordinate certain aspects of a project we are both working on; and visiting a site (usually at the very beginning of a project or at the very end).

—Landscape architect, 11 years,
Austin, Texas

. . .

What are the best parts of your profession?

Taking a raw piece of land and creating an overall design that not only meets the needs of the client but presents to the people who will ultimately live there an environment that will encourage their interaction with the land and with each other.

—Landscape architect, 18 years,
Knoxville, Tennessee

The most satisfying aspects of the profession are the creative aspects. For me, the more challenging the project, the more I enjoy it. With less and less land being developable, especially in urban settings, as a landscape architect I am being asked more and more frequently to work on projects that are centered around the reuse or regeneration of existing properties. The field of urban regeneration has for me opened up more interesting opportunities to apply my creativity.

—Landscape architect, 12 years,
Philadelphia, Pennsylvania

My recent certification in LEED has given my practice a reinvigoration. I was getting tired of doing one subdivision after another, and with LEED I can broaden my opportunities to apply my craft.

—Landscape architect, 9 years,
Charleston, South Carolina

. . .

What are the least enjoyable aspects of your profession?

The stress of deadlines.

—Landscape architect, 5 years,
Huntsville, Alabama

Having to always explain what I do to other people.

—Landscape architect, 3 years,
Springfield, Missouri

Dealing with the mentality of bureaucrats when you are seeking regulatory approval on projects from a planning commission, a zoning board, or a city planner.

—Landscape architect, 8 years,
Southhaven, Mississippi

CHANGES IN THE PROFESSION

What changes do you foresee for your profession?

The profession of landscape architecture is really beginning to shine right now. With the increase of environmental hurdles and regulations with which to comply, the demand for landscape architects is growing. We are not experts in any particular field, but rather we know something about a lot of different professions — engineering, construction, development, and planning. This broad knowledge base positions us well to be the point persons on a wide variety of projects as they are presented to various governmental bodies and agencies.

—Landscape architect, 7 years,
Nashville, Tennessee

As land that can be developed on a cost-efficient basis becomes less and less available, and as regulations for land use increase, the role of the landscape architect will become more essential. More engineering firms will start a landscape architecture division or expand their existing one, which means a favorable job outlook for new graduates in the near future.

—Landscape architect, 15 years,
Reston, Virginia

A much greater need for landscape architects to be LEED certified and to be knowledgeable about green building practices.

—Landscape architect, 11 years,
Shreveport, Louisiana

WOULD YOU DO IT ALL OVER AGAIN?

Do you find your daily job fulfilling?

Yes. I wish I had more time to be purely creative, but within the reality of making a living, looking forward to coming to work, and seeing your ideas come to fruition, landscape architecture has been a good fit for me.

—Landscape architect, 10 years,
Macon, Georgia

I started off on the traditional route of being the newest guy in a large urban firm. After several years of doing less and less of what I enjoyed, which was design work, and more and more project management, I started my own business with a couple of unique twists. I am doing much more straight design work, and at the same time I own my own retail garden and stone business, where my clients can come and see samples of the materials that will be part of their homes. This business model allows me to stay more involved with design work and with the actual end customer and also to have more than one source of revenue and profit.

—Landscape architect, 17 years,
Roswell, Georgia

Yes. I am busy enough that I get to work on several different-size projects each day, which gives me a diversity that has allowed the profession to remain reasonably fresh and engaging so far.

—Landscape architect, 8 years,
Germantown, Tennessee

. . .

Would you choose the same profession again?

Probably. There are times when I wish I had pursued architecture, but then I see a very creative individual who practices architecture whose days are spent designing basically the same school over and over again and on very tight budgets, and I realize I probably made the right choice.

—Landscape architect, 13 years,
St. Petersburg, Florida

If I had to do it all over again, I would choose real estate development. I know enough about all the various aspects, and usually a lot more than the clients I advise, who are making four or five times the annual income I am making.

—Landscape architect, 9 years,
Baltimore, Maryland

Yes, but I would have opened my firm with some partners much sooner.

—Landscape architect, 15 years,
Tigard, Oregon

A CAREER IN

The Law

SO YOU WANT TO BE AN ATTORNEY

I was most surprised by the almost immediate realization that law school doesn't prepare you for practicing law. Although it prepares you to think like an attorney (which I suppose is the most important aspect of being an attorney), it does not prepare you for the practical realities of practice. I have come to discover that nearly all attorneys (and certainly all transactional attorneys) agree with this sentiment.

The United States is a republic built upon laws, and the study and practice of law have been at the core of America since its inception. And yet, while there is an academic and interpretative theme that runs through all legal matters, the daily life of an attorney has as much or more to do with running a business and dealing with the everyday tribulations of all kinds of people under all kinds of circumstances.

As was the case for myself, most students get their ideas of what it is like to practice law from television and movies. For me, Gregory Peck in *To Kill a Mockingbird* personified the ideal lawyer, someone who, when faced with the worst of human behavior, represents his client with a resolute determination toward justice. However, as the book's author, Harper Lee, brilliantly discloses — justice does not always prevail.

Another inspiring film is *The Verdict*, starring Paul Newman, who portrays a flawed human being seeking justice not only for his client but to save his own soul. In this movie, the real hero is the law itself, the legal system, which provides the opportunity for justice. Then there are the television versions of the law, shows like *Law and Order* and *Boston Legal*. While *Boston Legal* is a self-consciously overdramatic version of practicing law, *Law and Order* succeeds by injecting as much realism as possible.

So what is it like to really be a lawyer? One thing for sure is that it is not all big cases and front-page headlines. There is a lot of tedium and repetition. Most of the work is performed behind the scenes and does not have the glamour or prestige that Hollywood or television portrays.

Examples of practicing attorneys include *criminal defense lawyers*, who defend people who are charged with a crime; *prosecuting attorneys*, who prosecute criminal cases for the government and represent the collective interests of the public; *trial attorneys*, who represent people who have been injured; *business attorneys*, who prepare contracts and other business documents; and *real estate attorneys*, who prepare leases and close real estate transactions.

The law is a very demanding profession for several reasons, and it suits those who thrive in high-pressure situations. First, an attorney's clients are often in stressful situations themselves, and they want solutions quickly. Practicing law is also done under the constant demands of government- and court-mandated deadlines and procedural rules, making the ability to collect and assess lots of information within a short time frame very important. Another thing to remember is that, by its very nature, the practice of law is adversarial, and this reality permeates the work climate of an attorney.

On the positive side, the practice of law can be a rewarding profession. Winning an important case for a client or successfully completing a difficult business negotiation is a very fulfilling experience. And the practice of law can be lucrative. Yet to make an excellent living at it, one must accept that the hours will be long, the pressure frequent, and the stress of dealing with antagonistic situations and people inevitable.

The practice of law has become a profession of specialization. Examples of areas of concentration include *bankruptcy*, *civil litigation*, *commercial transactions*, *corporate securities*, *criminal defense*, *employment and labor*, *entertainment*, *the environment*, *government relations*, *health care*, *intellectual property and technology*, *public finance*, *public prosecution*, *real estate*, *taxation*, and *telecommunications*. And within many of these areas of concentration are separate subspecialties. For example, in the area of litigation, attorneys may end up concentrating in such distinct subspecialties as antitrust, general business disputes, class actions, consumer protection, insurance defense, personal injury, products liability, and professional liability.

While there are still some general practitioners, and even a few solo practitioners, the vast majority within the legal profession practice law through partnerships. In these legal partnerships, attorneys with different specialties practice in the same office, with the more experienced attorneys becoming partners who divide the income from their collective efforts, and the less experienced attorneys acting as associates who are paid salaries as employees of the partnership.

The first step in a successful law career is to make the best grades possible in undergraduate school, thereby increasing your chances of being accepted by one of the top law schools. While there is no undergraduate major that is a prerequisite for law school, courses in pre-law and business traditionally give a law student a head start. Additionally, a high score on the nationally administered Law School Admission Test (LSAT) will also improve your chances of admission to your preferred law school.

There are currently 196 law schools that are approved by the American Bar Association (ABA). ABA approval is important because all states require a graduate to come from an ABA-approved law school before they can take the Bar Examination, which is a necessary step to securing a license to practice law. The Bar Exam is a nationally designed two-day examination; it consists of a multistate portion that covers all aspects of the law, followed by testing geared more to the law of the particular state where the exam is being administered.

Graduates from the top law schools historically can command the best salaries being offered year to year. To further enhance your chances of landing a well-paying job, it is recommended that you work part-time as a clerk with a law firm or for a local judge while attending law school. The academic demands of the three-year program are intense, and a part-time clerkship only adds to the pressure, but law firms look favorably on work experience because it places the graduate on a faster track to becoming an income-producing associate within the firm. After graduation, and while waiting to take the Bar Exam, associates work under the supervision of licensed attorneys within the firm.

BY THE NUMBERS

EMPLOYMENT LEVELS: According to the American Bar Association and the U.S. Bureau of Labor Statistics, the United States has over a million lawyers. Approximately 73 percent are practicing attorneys in private firms.

ACADEMIC REQUIREMENTS: A four-year undergraduate degree plus a three-year graduate degree are required to secure a doctor of jurisprudence (JD, or Juris Doctor). Before being allowed to practice, you must pass the nationally administered Bar Examination. Each state licenses attorneys practicing in the state, and the issue of reciprocity with other states varies from state to state.

AVERAGE SALARY LEVELS: According to the American Bar Association, starting salaries range from **$67,500** in firms of two to twenty-five attorneys to over **$125,000** in firms of more than five hundred lawyers. For firms of all sizes, the first-year median is **$100,000**, although first-year salaries also vary by region of the country. Partners in established law firms traditionally earn up to **$250,000** a year, and annual incomes of over **$1 MILLION** are not unheard of in the very large firms with offices in multiple cities.

COLLEGE VS. REALITY

How would you compare the reality of your profession to the picture you had of it while in school?

Get ready for reality. Practicing law has a lot to do with dealing with people who are under stress. You can't learn that in school. They don't care that you can quote the law on lots of topics. They just want you to win. Period.

—**Personal injury lawyer, 9 years, Los Angeles, California**

This is not like medical school, where you have an internship and a residency and loads of practical experience. If you go with a small firm, you have to jump in headfirst and start swimming against the current.

—**Criminal defense counsel, 2 years, Atlanta, Georgia**

I pictured a much less stressful day-to-day existence. I expected more academia, less procedural combat. In law school you don't have clients, just theories and facts that appear in books. It is like playing chess with no opponent and no time clock. There is no real pressure. The world does not work that way.

—**Trial attorney, 11 years, Schaumburg, Illinois**

. . .

How would you rate your collegiate and graduate courses in preparing you for your profession on a scale of 1 to 10, with 10 being the best?

Law school prepared me to think like an attorney, so I would give it an 8 or 9 in that respect, but failed to teach me how to practice law, so 3 to 4.

—**Insurance defense attorney, 12 years, Syracuse, New York**

Law school is all about how to think through a set of facts and then determine what is the right area of law to apply. It does not prepare you for dealing with judges, deadlines, and impatient clients.

**—Divorce attorney, 14 years,
Detroit, Michigan**

Don't expect college and even law school to prepare you for navigating the legal system. The best thing you can do is work in a legal clinic or clerk for a firm while in school.

**—Insurance defense lawyer, 20 years,
St. Louis, Missouri**

THE BIGGEST SURPRISE

What most surprised you about your chosen profession?

How much responsibility I was given, and how little law school prepared me for the practical aspects of such.

**—Criminal defense attorney, 1 year,
Memphis, Tennessee**

How competitive it was inside the firm among associates. Everyone is trying to kiss the most ass with the partners. There is a lot of jealousy and very little camaraderie.

**—Associate in seventy-lawyer firm, 2 years,
Philadelphia, Pennsylvania**

I was most surprised by the almost immediate realization that law school doesn't prepare you for practicing law. Although it prepares you to think like an attorney (which I suppose is the most important aspect of being an attorney), it does not prepare you for the practical realities of practice. I have come to discover that nearly all attorneys (and certainly all transactional attorneys) agree with this sentiment. I have found the most dramatic difference between law school and practicing law to be the shift in attitude away from gravitation to new and developing law and toward a repulsion of such areas, and a new gravitation toward reliable, solid precedent.

**—Business attorney, 3 years,
Greensboro, North Carolina**

HOURS AND ADVANCEMENT

How many hours do you work each week at your career?

It fluctuates, but a low of sixty hours a week to a high of one hundred.

**—Associate in midsize business firm,
3 years, Washington, D.C.**

Seventy hours a week.

**—Bankruptcy attorney, 10 years,
Chicago, Illinois**

You work whatever number of hours it takes to win. Right before trial that can be a hundred hours a week. But lots of cases settle, and you may be able to take two days off unexpectedly the next week.

—Trial attorney, 6 years, Jacksonville, Florida

. . .

Have you found advancement within your career easy or difficult?

The typical track for attorneys in mid- to large-size firms is as an associate for five to nine years before being invited to become a partner in the firm. I found the learning curve to be long but natural.

—Associate in sixty-five-lawyer business firm, 6 years, Seattle, Washington

Billable hours are the standard. You bill the requisite hours, you advance; you don't, you won't.

—Associate in thirty-lawyer firm, 5 years, Richmond, Virginia

Screw the eight-to-ten-year associate-to-partner route. Learn everything you can the first five years, and then find some equally confident and productive attorneys, and start your own firm where everyone starts off as a partner.

—Partner in seven-lawyer business firm, 6 years, St. Louis, Missouri

THE BEST AND THE WORST

What do you spend most of your day doing? Describe a typical day.

As a real estate attorney, I spend the majority preparing documents for closings or drafting new contracts for the more complicated commercial sales, along with representing my clients in phone conversations or via email as regards the negotiation of various issues in property sales or acquisitions.

—Real estate attorney, 14 years, Trenton, New Jersey

My days are spent drafting pleadings, responding to interrogatories, conducting depositions, arguing motions, trying cases, and negotiating settlements on behalf of my litigation clients.

—Trial attorney, 11 years, Austin, Texas

I practice corporate law, which means that I am drafting various business agreements, participating in meetings with clients and their nonlegal advisors, reviewing internal client business documentation in an effort to assess possible legal risks, and advising clients on the sale of their assets.

—Business attorney, 16 years, Troy, Michigan

. . .

What are the best parts of your profession?

Being part of capitalism. Helping to get the deals closed and being well paid for it. Those are the best parts of my job.

—Commercial real estate attorney, 12 years, Boston, Massachusetts

Connecting with a jury is the best aspect of my trial practice. Having the opportunity to let real citizens decide what damages are fair for your client, and then the huge fees you can earn when victorious.

—**Personal injury lawyer, 20 years,**
Tampa, Florida

The intellectual challenge that the law presents you. The law is a constantly evolving body of knowledge, and the person with the best understanding of that information usually is able to apply it most advantageously. Law is to some degree like a massive chess game, but with real people involved.

—**Defense attorney, 16 years,**
Little Rock, Arkansas

...

What are the least enjoyable aspects of your profession?

The reputation in the business community of attorneys is not the one I envisioned in school. It turns out most people don't like lawyers, viewing them only as a necessary evil.

—**Labor law attorney, 4 years, Topeka, Kansas**

The worst part is the time it takes to get to the end of any contested matter. The reality of the legal system is that it feeds on controversy. If you are impatient and like quick results, you may make good money, but you will be a frustrated SOB.

—**Business trial attorney, 14 years,**
Knoxville, Tennessee

The worst part is the endless deadlines caused by the rules of procedure. It means lots of weekend work, and unless you have a great support staff, the inability to completely escape for two weeks.

—**Civil trial attorney, 7 years,**
Chattanooga, Tennessee

CHANGES IN THE PROFESSION

What changes do you foresee for your profession?

The profession will continue to become more "corporate" in orientation — not corporate law but culture — small firms merging into large firms, and large firms merging interstate into regional and national organizations that have CFOs, marketing departments, and elaborate information and accounting systems.

—**Business attorney, 28 years,**
Brentwood, Tennessee

It has become a business rather than a profession. Associates at the large firms are robots that must grind out the hours; the attitude eventually impacts everyone: no respect, hard attitudes, lack of professional courtesy.

—**Business trial attorney, 30 years,**
Nashville, Tennessee

A major change and one that will continue to permeate the law is computer technology. Overall it has been a positive thing, especially for research.

—Insurance defense attorney, 22 years,
Phoenix, Arizona

WOULD YOU DO IT ALL OVER AGAIN?

Do you find your daily job fulfilling?

The law can have a positive effect on society. It can force entire industries to clean up their dangerous practices. The little man needs someone to stand up for him. I like the challenge of taking on the soulless corporate world. The law levels the playing field.

—Personal injury attorney, 15 years,
Dallas, Texas

I find my job very fulfilling. I help our clients achieve their largest goals. So far it has not been boring. I believe I will do this until they carry me out.

—Associate in private finance firm, 5 years,
Milwaukee, Wisconsin

No. They say that the law is a jealous mistress. My wife concurs. I am rarely home, miss most of my children's weekend sports activities, and am virtually always on call to help put out whatever fire the partner decides is burning the hottest. At first it was an academic ego trip, seeing if I could outsmart the other side and win favor with my bosses. After the third year, I realized that if I dropped dead, there would

be a dozen more young associates waiting to take my place.

—Associate in eighty-lawyer firm, 4 years,
Washington, D.C.

...

Would you choose the same profession again?

I definitely would not choose the legal profession again. I spend eighty hours a week, including most weekends, working on cases the partners don't care to deal with. I have no life outside work. I would choose a career that would allow me to have a more balanced life and work on things that interest me.

—Associate in sixty-lawyer firm, 5 years,
Chicago, Illinois

I would choose to be a doctor instead. People need doctors. They view lawyers as a necessary evil.

—Associate in business defense firm, 6 years,
Orlando, Florida

You can make a good living practicing law, but if I had to do it all over again, I would choose something I had more control over, and that was less stressful and yet had the potential for great monetary rewards, such as venture capitalism or commercial real estate development. In the law, every time you try to push forward, there is someone on the other side who is pushing back. The endless tug-of-war gets old pretty quickly.

—Business trial attorney, 10 years,
Portland, Oregon

CAREERS IN

Accounting and Financial Services

SO YOU WANT TO BE AN ACCOUNTANT

Jobs for accountants should be quite abundant in the future because of a number of factors. The tax laws continue to change frequently, and that results in more required review by public accountants to always assure compliance. At the same time, as a result of the Enron, WorldCom, and other scandals, the demand for audits has increased dramatically. Every governmental organization and every nonprofit is now being audited on a more regular basis. That is not to say that accounting jobs will not continue to be outsourced to India, as has been occurring across our industry. However, I see the outsourced jobs as being centered around the actual bookkeeping aspects of the profession, and the new jobs as being directed toward management and consulting services within a more specialized framework.

Like engineers, accountants get a bad rap. The popular image is of a detail-obsessed, conservative, risk-averse person hunched for hours (if not days) over dull spreadsheets and columns of numbers, adding them up and analyzing the results, all to create more spreadsheets. However, as the old saying goes, "you can't judge a book by its cover." For instance, the 2003 winner of the World Series of Poker was Chris Moneymaker, an accountant by day and a poker player by night. He might be detail obsessed, but he definitely likes to take risks.

Another misperception about accountants is that they are merely pencil pushers, glorified bookkeepers who simply move figures from debit columns to credit columns and back again. On the contrary, the world of accountancy is a much more diverse and influential profession. Accountants are a key link between lenders and borrowers; they are relied on to accurately assess a borrower's financial condition, without which banks could not manage the risks of lending money, without which businesses could not get the working capital they need to function. Accountants convert the messy real world into facts and figures that allow for meaningful, apple-to-apple comparisons, and they present this in a uniformly established, agreed-upon reporting format.

As for the profession itself, while all certified public accountants (CPAs) are accountants, not all public accountants are CPAs. The requirements to become a certified public accountant vary by state, and the certification is not always transferrable between states. To become a CPA, you need an undergraduate degree in accounting, you need to pass the Uniform CPA Examination, and then you must obtain a specific amount of professional work experience in public accounting (the amount varies by state).

Accountants go by different titles. Those involved in offering their services to the public are known as *certified public accountants*; those maintaining and examining records for government agencies, or for businesses or individuals doing business with the government, are known as *government accountants*; and those who record and analyze the financial information of the companies for which they work are known as *management accountants* (also referred to as *industrial*, *corporate*, and *private accountants*).

In public practice, CPAs are hired by individual clients and provide services like accounting, auditing, cash-flow projections, tax return preparation and consulting, business valuation, management consulting, financial planning, and technology consulting. CPAs employed in business, industry, and government are responsible for accounting and financial reporting, implementing and managing internal accounting controls and information systems, and compliance with tax laws and regulations.

One of the newest specialties is forensic accounting and litigation services. Forensic accountants are hired to uncover the misdeeds of unscrupulous business owners or individuals — those who may be hiding assets or misappropriating revenues, or perhaps laundering money, falsifying or destroying financial records, or committing cyber theft. The importance of forensic accounting came to the nation's attention with the Enron scandal, in which false financial reporting and other massive financial irregularities caused the downfall of the Houston-based energy company (once named "America's Most Innovative Company" by *Forbes* magazine).

The collapse of Enron also caused the demise of its public accounting firm, Arthur Andersen, at that time one of the world's "Big Five" accounting firms. After being indicted on federal fraud charges and obstruction of justice, Arthur Andersen went from eighty-five thousand employees worldwide to less than three thousand. The image of public accounting also received a black eye, particularly when the Enron scandal was followed by the financial mischief that engulfed WorldCom, Tyco, Adelphia, and others. However, with time and new federal regulations, the world of accountancy has returned to its more staid image of examining, analyzing, and interpreting financial reports.

The American Institute of Certified Public Accountants, which was founded in 1887, now has more than 330,000 members. There are over half a million CPAs in the United States, and women make up 56 percent of new public accountants. The influence of women in accounting has created better balances between work and life needs, and this has meant the creation of more part-time partners and non-partnership career tracks.

Major accounting firms have a definite structural hierarchy. From top to bottom, they are made up of partners/shareholders, senior managers, managers, supervisors, and staff accountants. Many large firms have a separate director of tax and director of audit. In smaller firms and individual practices, the business structure mirrors the two-tier systems of smaller law firms, with partners and associates. In business and industry, the role of accountant is seen as that of corporate officer.

Traditionally, an aptitude for mathematics is a prerequisite for a career as an accountant, along with developing a good working knowledge of economic and accounting principles. However, being computer savvy is now also a major plus, as information technology is changing the daily life of accountants. Some CPAs are now electing to become certified as information technology professionals (CITP), while other specialty certifications include becoming accredited in business valuations (ABV) and as personal financial specialists (PFS).

BY THE NUMBERS

EMPLOYMENT LEVELS: According to the American Institute of Certified Public Accountants, there are over 500,000 CPAs practicing in the United States. If you add those participating as accountants and auditors in government, tax preparation services, bookkeeping, and payroll services, the total number increases to over 1.2 million.

ACADEMIC REQUIREMENTS: The requirements for becoming a certified public accountant are becoming more stringent. An undergraduate degree in accounting is, and has always been, a requirement, but now almost every state has increased the number of total undergraduate hours to 150. In response, many colleges and universities are now offering a master's in accounting. In addition to completing the academic work, all CPAs must pass the four-part Uniform CPA Exam. To ensure that would-be CPAs complete what are known as the Three E's (education, examination, and experience), many states require a certain period of experience working in the field of public accounting before one can be designated as a CPA.

AVERAGE SALARY LEVELS: According to the U.S. Bureau of Labor Statistics, the median salary for all accountants is **$50,770**; the range of average salaries is from **$32,320** to **$88,610**. The starting salary for a junior accountant with the federal government is **$24,677**; once junior accountants have two years of working experience, the average government salary rises to **$37,390**. According to the National Association of Colleges and Employers, starting salaries in the public sector, depending on the city and the size of the firm, average **$43,269** for those with a degree in accounting and **$46,251** for those with a master's in accounting.

COLLEGE VS. REALITY

How would you compare the reality of your profession to the picture you had of it while in school?

The profession is much more people oriented than I anticipated. In school you are learning in the abstract. They are just figures. Once you get in the real world, all the figures have a face or group of faces connected to them. You are no longer dealing with just numbers. Now people's personalities and work habits are interjected into the mix, and the whole thing changes.

—CPA, 5 years, New Haven, Connecticut

School can never fully prepare you for what the real world is like. However, with public accounting, the nature of the profession, with its uniform accounting practices, allows you to anticipate the basic framework in which you will be applying your knowledge. The part of the profession that I did not fully anticipate or appreciate was the community involvement necessary to obtain a growing list of clients.

—CPA, 7 years, Muncie, Indiana

My picture of the world of accounting has turned out to be pretty accurate, but then I knew I wanted to enter the world of private accounting. I did not want to deal with various clients with a diverse list of problems. Rather, I wanted to master a more controlled corporate setting, where I could be aware of everything financial that came in and went out.

—Management accountant, 12 years, Boston, Massachusetts

. . .

How would you rate your collegiate and graduate courses in preparing you for your profession on a scale of 1 to 10, with 10 being the best?

I have a degree in accounting, so my preparation was relatively good. However, I wish I had taken more legal courses, in that, as a CPA, I seem to be asked as many legal questions as accounting questions. Not that I can per se give legal advice, but the legal implications of certain actions by clients have a direct impact on the options that we can pursue, and by understanding the law better, I would be more effective for my clients.

—CPA, 11 years, Owensboro, Kentucky

My accounting degree did a good job in giving me the basics, but the day-to-day world of public accounting is nothing like what I learned in school. There is no substitute for job experience, which brings you into the real world, with real people and real consequences.

—CPA, 7 years, Garden Grove, California

You can only learn so much in school. I highly recommend internships or junior accountant positions to introduce you to the flow within a CPA's office. There is a necessary rhythm that has to occur between gathering information, compiling the information, and then presenting the information in the structured and official formats.

—CPA, 12 years, Fort Wayne, Indiana

THE BIGGEST SURPRISE

What most surprised you about your chosen profession?

The high turnover rate among young accountants. Statistics from the American Institute of CPAs, which reflect a turnover rate of 30 percent, seem to bear out what we have experienced when trying to hire new associates. Once I decided I wanted to be a CPA, I looked forward to staying in one community, building my practice, raising my family, and becoming a permanent part of my city. Graduates today seem to approach accounting from a different perspective — almost like they chose this career by default.

—CPA, 18 years, Stockton, California

The fact that I could grow from an accounting position with my company into a more managerial role of helping to run the company on a day-to-day basis.

—CFO, 14 years, Naperville, Illinois

How many other women are choosing the field of accountancy. I think our collective presence will help transform the profession for the better, with the implementation of a more flexible work-week to accommodate raising a family and working from home part of the time.

—CPA, 5 years, Corpus Christi, Texas

HOURS AND ADVANCEMENT

How many hours do you work each week at your career?

Easily fifty-plus a week, and then with tax season that can explode to eighty a week.

—CPA, 15 years, Mobile, Alabama

I work a full week of fifty to fifty-five hours, and that does not include taking work home at least once a week.

—CPA, 9 years, Louisville, Kentucky

Fifty-five to sixty hours. There is always a file I need to be working on, and the nature of accountancy is such that we always have major deadlines to keep in mind. And at the same time, most people who request our services are anxious to see the final numbers so they can use them to advance another business goal.

—CPA/staff accountant, 8 years,
Ft. Lauderdale, Florida

. . .

Have you found advancement within your career easy or difficult?

Easy. There is a steady demand for experienced CPAs.

—Supervisor, regional accounting firm,
12 years, Alpharetta, Georgia

The more frequent changes in tax laws and the broader application across more industries of required periodic audits have resulted in a need for qualified CPAs, so if you are good at your work, you can advance within this profession.

—CPA, 6 years, Baton Rouge, Louisiana

The term "advance" has to be defined. If you are talking about moving up within a large national or regional firm, there are always the ego and personality dynamics to deal with that are found within any large corporate structure. If you are one of the self-employed accountants building their own practice, advancement comes with clients and increased billings. I have been in both environments, and while I learned an immense amount within the large corporate enterprise, I am much more fulfilled captaining my own ship.

—CPA, 15 years, Tempe, Arizona

THE BEST AND THE WORST

What do you spend most of your day doing? Describe a typical day.

I spend less and less time working with figures. Luckily, I have two young associates who have taken up the slack for me. A good portion of my average day is spent in meetings with clients or their other professional representatives. Over the years my practice has evolved into more business management consulting and financial planning in conjunction with others representing my long-term clients.

—CPA, 25 years, Providence, Rhode Island

It depends on the time of year, but on a given day, I could be doing general bookkeeping (compiling a set of books for a client), taking a client's books and making adjustments to complete their tax return, preparing payroll tax returns, compiling financial statements (monthly, quarterly, or annual), preparing business tax returns, preparing individual tax returns, doing tax research, or responding to IRS notices clients receive.

—CPA, 16 years, Brentwood, Tennessee

My day is usually a mix of working in different aspects of the field of public accounting. That could include a client whose business we have been asked to value, preparing an audit for one of the governmental agencies in my community, consulting with clients on the best way to handle a particular issue within their businesses, working with others in my office on the tax returns for our corporate clients, advising investors on the best way to structure a new real estate development, or updating myself on the latest tax letters and rulings on the continually changing tax laws and standards.

—CPA, 21 years, Rome, Georgia

. . .

What are the best parts of your profession?

Assisting clients with proper planning to avoid costly estate tax burdens derivative from wealth that they had accumulated through decades of hard work or fortuitous real estate appreciation.

—CPA, 15 years, Plano, Texas

Seeing my role as an advisor truly benefit small businesses as they grow into much larger companies.

—CPA, 18 years, Lexington, Kentucky

The opportunities to learn new things and become certified in newly emerging areas of specialty as the world of public accountancy changes and evolves. They have allowed me to grow within my profession, helping to keep it fresh and engaging as the years tick by at an alarmingly brisk pace.

—CPA, 22 years, Cincinnati, Ohio

. . .

What are the least enjoyable aspects of your profession?

The stress and exceedingly long hours during tax season.

—CPA, 17 years, Rochester, New York

As a young accountant for a national accounting firm, I at first found the travel to distant cities to tackle a new assignment exciting. After several years of frequent travel, living in hotels, and often being engaged as a necessary evil, I long for a stable day-to-day life within a smaller office environment, which lends itself to more permanent relationships with my coworkers and my clients.

—CPA/auditor, 4 years, Atlanta, Georgia

Being viewed as the enemy when I am just doing my job.

—Government auditor, banking industry, 12 years, Washington, D.C.

CHANGES IN THE PROFESSION

What changes do you foresee for your profession?

There will continue to be more and more consolidation as larger firms purchase smaller firms, or small firms form alliances so they can compete with the larger firms. The era of the true general practice of public accounting is about over. Specialization is the direction the practice has been heading, and that trend will only increase.

—CPA, 14 years, Greenville, South Carolina

The profession is changing in that accountants are being asked to provide more and more management and business advice, and less and less the straight bookkeeping services.

—CPA, 17 years, Tulsa, Oklahoma

Jobs for accountants should be quite abundant in the future because of a number of factors. The tax laws continue to change frequently, and that results in more required review by public accountants to always assure compliance. At the same time, as a result of the Enron, WorldCom, and other scandals, the demand for audits has increased dramatically. Every governmental organization and every nonprofit is now being audited on a more regular basis. That is not to say that accounting jobs will not continue to be outsourced to India, as has been occurring across our industry. However, I see the outsourced jobs as being centered around the actual bookkeeping aspects of the profession, and the new jobs being directed toward management and consulting services within a more specialized framework.

—CPA, 43 years, Franklin, Tennessee

WOULD YOU DO IT ALL OVER AGAIN?

Do you find your daily job fulfilling?

Public accounting has been a good first job after college. It has caused me to be much more disciplined in my business affairs than I would have been otherwise, and it has allowed me the opportunity to see how a wide variety of businesses operate. Is it something I want to do forever? No. I want to find my own entrepreneurial niche.

—**Staff accountant, regional accounting firm, 4 years, Richmond, Virginia**

After several years in public accounting, I started to get burned out. What has allowed me to have a new enjoyment is the new specialty of forensic accounting, in which I am now spending most of my time. It is not *CSI*, but I am helping catch the bad guys.

—**CPA/forensic accountant, 12 years, Las Vegas, Nevada**

Yes. Other things have interested me from time to time, but overall I cannot think of anything that would give me the satisfaction this profession does. I first worked in private accounting, and it became rather boring. Public accounting has allowed me to grow within my profession and to interact with and assist a wide variety of interesting individuals within a broad business environment.

—**CPA/CITP, 16 years, Birmingham, Alabama**

. . .

Would you choose the same profession again?

Yes, but I would probably choose to work as an accountant in the private sector, which is much more stable and has less demanding hours as a whole.

—**CPA, 11 years, Charlotte, North Carolina**

No. If I had to do it all over again, I would go into the law, with maybe an LLM in taxation. I find myself frequently asked legal questions, but I am not permitted to give legal advice. With a law degree, specializing in taxation, I could expand my opportunity for greater income.

—**CPA, 16 years, Tacoma, Washington**

Being a CPA is not the most exciting profession, but our economy, banking structure, and tax laws have always created a need for our services. We are paid reasonably well for our knowledge of issues that are not as complex as can be found in other professions, and the industry offers employment opportunities for those who want to remain employees and for those who want to be entrepreneurs. Not a bad gig overall.

—**CPA, 9 years, Colorado Springs, Colorado**

SO YOU WANT TO BE A BANKER

From the very beginning, I was most surprised to learn that almost every single employee has to meet sales goals — whether to open so many new accounts each month, to make a certain number of cold calls to businesses in the community, or, for those authorized to make loans, to achieve a certain number or dollar amount of new loans. Banking is really a sales job — you are just selling financial products.

Banking in the United States is constantly evolving. Dramatic changes began in the 1970s, and these have continued through the computer revolution, which has remade many bank services. How could we function today without ATMs, automatic deposits, and online banking?

The profession of banking actually predates the invention of money, when deposits consisted of goods and, later, precious metals. Banking occurred in ancient Rome and Greece, with loans, deposits, currency exchange, and extensions of credit. The word "bank" is derived from the Italian word *banco*, or *banca*, which means "bench" or "desk." This is because Italian bankers conducting business in public places seated themselves at benches to write their letters, count their money, or draw their bills of exchange.

In the simplest terms a bank is a business that offers financial services for a profit. The U.S. Bank Holding Company Act of 1956 defines a bank as any depository financial institution that accepts checking accounts (checks) or makes commercial loans, and whose deposits are insured by a federal deposit insurance agency. A bank acts as a middleman between suppliers of funds and users of funds; banks substitute their own credit judgment for that of the suppliers of funds, and banks collect funds from three sources: checking accounts, savings accounts, and time deposits; short-term borrowings from other banks; and equity capital. In the United States, banking's central function has traditionally been to put a community's surplus funds (in the form of deposits and investments) to work by lending these funds to people in the community to purchase homes and cars, to start and expand businesses, to put their children through college, and for countless other purposes.

This traditional role of banking continued as the norm from the end of World War II until the late 1970s. In the 1980s and 1990s the banking industry began moving into a broader-based business model offering more diverse services. This was a response to globalization, as large companies dealt with customers, suppliers, manufacturers, and information centers around the world. With historically low interest rates in the last part of the twentieth century, banks began looking for additional ways to generate profits.

Such growing internationalization and opportunity in financial services has entirely changed the competitive landscape, as now many banks have demonstrated a preference for the universal banking model so prevalent in Europe. Universal banks are free to engage in all forms of financial services, and they function as much as possible as a one-stop supplier of both retail and wholesale financial services. This growth and opportunity have also led to an unexpected outcome: the entrance into the market of other financial intermediaries, or nonbanks. Large corporate players began to find their way into the financial service community, offering competition to established banks. The main products offered include insurance, pension funds, mutual funds, money market and hedge funds, loans, credit, and securities.

This means consumers can get banking services from many different financial institutions, and many of the key functional distinctions between commercial banks and investment banking companies have disappeared. Commercial banks are now permitted to deal in securities, offer investment advice, sell insurance and other products, and perform other functions related to banking through subsidiary companies.

If you're considering employment as a banker, the evolution of the banking world has produced several central themes to keep in mind. One is that through consolidation banks are becoming larger and larger. As of 2000, the top ten banks in the world commanded a market share of 80 percent. The odds are that even if you are working for a small local bank branch, it will most likely be tied to a large corporation and have all the corporation's internal rules and regulations.

Also, with technology removing the traditional boundaries between financial institutions and services, banks are competing more with each other for business. This means that bank employees are expected to spend part of their time developing new business. The days of waiting for new customers to simply walk through the door are over. Increasingly, a bank's income depends on the fees charged for its various services (rather than just from interest on loans), making new accounts essential.

There is a diverse array of occupations within the banking industry, including *executives, operations managers, financial managers, accountants and auditors, credit analysts, financial analysts, loan officers, personal financial advisors*, and *financial examiners*. For all, you need to have good math skills, be technologically savvy, be able to deal with many sets of financial regulations, and have good interpersonal skills. Odds are you will start out in a branch, and you must be willing to make cold calls on new businesses. While banks certainly still deal with checking and savings accounts and with personal and business loans, becoming a banker today to a large extent involves sales. It is now customary for bank employees to have monthly quotas for new accounts, number of mortgage loans, and so on. Your products are the services your bank offers, and your ability to move up within the banking profession will depend greatly on how much new business you can generate.

BY THE NUMBERS

EMPLOYMENTS LEVELS: According to the U.S. Bureau of Labor Statistics, there are 1,783,000 individuals employed by banks in the United States. Of these nearly 1.2 million are in office and administrative support occupations (bookkeeping, tellers, customer service, credit authorizers, secretaries, and administrative assistants). According to the Federal Deposit Insurance Corporation, there are currently over nine thousand banks in the United States, which range in size from less than $100 million in deposits to over $50 billion.

ACADEMIC REQUIREMENTS: There are no specific educational requirements for a career in banking. However, in today's world, a college degree is a must, and it's helpful to have taken courses in finance, accounting, economics, and business. However, there is heavy competition for good people, so many banks have strong in-house training programs, which allows individuals with no financial experience to successfully work their way up from teller to branch manager. For both federally and state-chartered banks, there are professional courses, conducted by the American Bankers Association in conjunction with certain universities, that allow working bankers to achieve accreditation in particular aspects of banking operations. The largest banking companies and international banking houses look for MBA graduates from some of the nation's top graduate schools to fill financial management and executive roles.

AVERAGE SALARY LEVELS: Salaries differ greatly depending on one's job and the bank's location in the country. As examples, according to the U.S. Bureau of Labor Statistics, financial managers average **$76,000**, loan officers **$47,500**, and tellers **$21,000**.

COLLEGE VS. REALITY

How would you compare the reality of your profession to the picture you had of it while in school?

My educational degree was in marketing, so what I am doing now is completely different from what I saw myself doing after college. I understood that I would be starting in a branch bank environment, and so what I do on a daily basis is what I anticipated I would do. Although you are dealing with finances, banking at the branch level is about helping people achieve their financial and business goals and assisting them in their daily finances and checking accounts.

—**Assistant branch manager, 3 years,**
Muncie, Indiana

I envisioned banking to be walnut-paneled boardrooms, private dining rooms, and multimillion-dollar deals. You can attain all of that, but not before paying your dues in the trenches of checking accounts, overdrafts, and auto loans. It can take fifteen years to reach the inner sanctum of structuring major development loans and corporate expansions. The key is attracting business. The person who can bring in the most business rises up the ladder the fastest.

—**Senior vice president, commercial lending,**
21 years, Tucson, Arizona

If you start in banking at the branch level, rather than in one of the corporate departments such as commercial real estate, financial management, or loan underwriting, it is immaterial what picture you have of banking, because it is about having endless patience with people of all types, many of whom are stressed when they come to see you, following strict documentation procedures, constantly trying to get new business, and overseeing your staff, which has a high turnover rate.

—Branch manager, 6 years,
Colorado Springs, Colorado

. . .

How would you rate your collegiate and graduate courses in preparing you for your profession on a scale of 1 to 10, with 10 being the best?

College only teaches you the financial world in broad strokes, unless you go on and get your MBA. Banking is customer driven, and having the right contacts after graduation can be as important as what you know about balance sheets and cash flow.

—Commercial loan officer, 16 years,
Cincinnati, Ohio

A 5. I took courses in accountancy and financing, which gave me a good background, but until you have a borrower walk through the door, or, more realistically, you bring the borrower through your door, you can't apply what you know.

—Vice president/branch manager, 9 years,
Gainesville, Florida

Only on-the-job experience allows you to understand how your customer's business works, whether it is manufacturing, auto sales, or home construction. You have to learn how to structure a loan that allows your customer to succeed, so he can repay you on a timely basis. You don't learn that in school.

—Construction loan officer,
14 years, Houston, Texas

THE BIGGEST SURPRISE

What most surprised you about your chosen profession?

From the very beginning, I was most surprised to learn that almost every single employee has to meet sales goals — whether to open so many new accounts each month, to make a certain number of cold calls to businesses in the community, or, for those authorized to make loans, to achieve a certain number or dollar amount of new loans. Banking is really a sales job — you are just selling financial products.

—Assistant branch manager,
4 years, Paterson, New Jersey

I anticipated that my daily business matters would be of greater consequence than covering overdrafts, making change for retailers, handling deposits, and opening accounts.

—Teller at branch bank, 1 year,
Richmond, Kentucky

How many different financial products you have to learn about, including mortgages and insurance. Banking has become a one-stop shop for a business, and you have to wear many different hats. Also surprising was the cutthroat competition among local and national banks in your community.

—Assistant branch manager, 3 years, Chattanooga, Tennessee

HOURS AND ADVANCEMENT

How many hours do you work each week at your career?

Forty-five to fifty.

—Branch manager, 10 years, Tulsa, Oklahoma

Forty-five.

—Loan officer, 9 years, Scottsboro, Alabama

Fifty.

—Commercial banker, 15 years, Syracuse, New York

. . .

Have you found advancement within your career easy or difficult?

It's easy if you want to stay in a branch, but if you want to work in other departments of the bank, the going can be slow because people are entrenched in those positions for years.

—Branch manager, 5 years, Provo, Utah

It all boils down to business. If you are bringing in consistently good new business (loans that do not default), you can advance within the bank. However, generally, advancement is made difficult by outside industry forces — consolidation and automation — that decrease the opportunities for jobs in the banking industry.

—Commercial loan officer, 17 years, Hartford, Connecticut

More difficult than I anticipated. Once people achieve jobs in higher-salaried positions, they tend to stay in them because, with all the consolidation between banks, they are afraid to go back out in the marketplace looking for alternate banking positions. Openings for the great positions with one's own bank are therefore rare.

—Financial manager, 9 years, Mobile, Alabama

THE BEST AND THE WORST

What do you spend most of your day doing? Describe a typical day.

Every day is different, but my weekly activities usually include dealing directly with customers, supervising staff, calling on prospective new accounts in the community, and communicating with other departments in the bank to facilitate and monitor the processing of new business.

—Branch manager, 6 years,
Virginia Beach, Virginia

Managing account relationships, underwriting commercial real estate transactions, cross-selling bank products, and portfolio management.

—Commercial real estate banker, 12 years,
Atlanta, Georgia

Reviewing loan applications and supportive documentation and communicating with loan officers in several states as to concerns regarding new loans.

—Credit analyst, 9 years, Tampa, Florida

. . .

What are the best parts of your profession?

The best part of being a banker is making a deal work for your customer and for the bank. Traditionally, bankers have had a reputation for being conservative, and while the requirements for approvals are designed to be rigorous, philosophically many bankers have to be progressive because of strong competition for business. To make the most income for the bank, bankers have

to have the most money at work. To achieve that, they want to close the most deals.

—Senior vice president, 25 years,
Dallas, Texas

Being able to achieve a level of specialization when working for a large multistate banking institution rather than having to wear as many hats as when I worked for a small local bank.

—Commercial real estate officer, 18 years,
Philadelphia, Pennsylvania

Helping people achieve their personal and business goals and the long-term personal relationships I have made.

—Executive vice president, 29 years,
Jackson, Mississippi

. . .

What are the least enjoyable aspects of your profession?

The frequent meetings, training sessions, and other required activities outside the bank that take up time but inhibit you from completing the level of business that your superiors are demanding you achieve.

—Loan officer, 8 years, Omaha, Nebraska

The uncertainty of your future with the company. Working in banking can be a lot like gambling at times. You have to weigh your options of approving something outside of policy for the sake of a client relationship. I've seen many bank employees make a poor decision that has cost them their job.

—Branch manager inside retail store,
3 years, Nashville, Tennessee

The fact that your consolidations of both intrastate and interstate banks are going to continue, and unless you are way up the corporate ladder, your job can be gone in a flash when your bank merges or is purchased. There is no loyalty. It is all about how much income the assets of the bank are making.

—Commercial loan officer, 7 years,
Jacksonville, Florida

CHANGES IN THE PROFESSION

What changes do you foresee for your profession?

More and more consolidation of banks, which will make the competition for jobs that much more difficult.

—Commercial loan officer, 14 years,
Anaheim, California

Increased competition between banks for clients, and more mega banks coming on the scene.

—Banker inside retail store, 2 years,
Brentwood, Tennessee

A continued shift to longer bank hours and more days open, as customers want

banks that are convenient. So more in-store branches and retailers like Wal-Mart getting into the banking business.

—Branch manager inside retail store,
5 years, Baltimore, Maryland

WOULD YOU DO IT ALL OVER AGAIN?

Do you find your daily job fulfilling?

On a daily basis I like my job because no two days are alike, and I am a people person and like helping people. But I don't find it that fulfilling as a career because I can't overcome the industry's advancement limitations, and it's hard to stay stimulated in my job.

—Loan officer, 8 years, Wilmington, Delaware

No, not really. I interact with people who think I have all this authority to help them with their business loans and needs, but I am just a conduit. I am farming out all the real analysis to people with the bank in other states, who I never even meet. Many days I feel like a clerk at the airline ticket counter — I rarely get to board the plane, much less fly it.

—Branch manager, 5 years,
Charleston, South Carolina

It is okay for now. I am twenty-seven, and I have a better job than most of my friends, but this is not going to be a career for me. Too many people above me looking over my shoulder waiting for me to screw up.

—Assistant branch manager, 3 years, Birmingham, Alabama

. . .

Would you choose the same profession again?

No. I would open my own business so I could make my own decisions, rather than basically being a conduit between the customer and the decision maker in some office in another state, who never meets the customer but is relying on my paperwork to decide whether to make a loan.

—Branch manager, 7 years, Bristol, Virginia

No. I would choose a profession where I controlled my own destiny more.

—Loan officer, 9 years, Rockford, Illinois

Yes. Each day is different, and I meet lots of interesting people from various walks of life, who call on me to help them with small and large problems. Plus the health and retirement benefits are good.

—Branch manager, 18 years, Paducah, Kentucky

SO YOU WANT TO BE A FINANCIAL PLANNER

My day usually starts at 6 AM, when I begin reading several different general and financial newspapers to get a sense of what is happening in the world. I am constantly monitoring the markets throughout the day as well as meeting with clients. My average client is around sixty-five, and I meet with each of them at least twice a year, unless circumstances dictate more frequent meetings. I try to take a midday break for a few hours for nourishment and exercise and then am back at studying and monitoring investment trends and being as actively involved in the markets as the needs of my clients dictate. My day ends around 9 PM, after I watch the last of several financial reports and shows on MSNBC and other networks.

Financial planners, as the name suggests, assist individuals in planning their financial future. Financial planners are also often referred to as financial advisors, but these are not official titles. From a legal and regulatory view, a financial planner is different from an investment advisor representative or registered investment advisor, which is the official term used by states and regulatory bodies for anyone who charges a fee for investment advice. And then there are broker-dealers, which is the official term for those who charge for the purchase and sale of securities.

Financial planners now work in a wide variety of settings and companies. Some work as sales agents for insurance companies like Mass

Mutual or Northwestern Mutual. Some financial companies, like American Express, offer the services of their own in-house financial advisors, as do large brokerage firms like Merrill Lynch, whose commercials urge you to contact one of their financial advisors to plan for your retirement. Large national and regional banks, like Bank of America and Wachovia, also advertise their financial planning expertise.

Over two decades ago, banks, brokerage firms, and insurance companies quietly began merging their offerings and becoming one-stop shops for their clients and customers. In part, they reasoned, why lose the fees and income that a client's related financial needs could generate? Now, many offer a full range of money and asset management, retirement planning, brokerage products, and insurance. Today, most banks, brokerage houses, and insurance companies refer to themselves as members of the financial services industry. This combined industry constitutes the largest group of companies in the world in terms of earnings and overall capitalized stock value.

In addition, there is an ever-increasing array of investments and financial options available in the marketplace. For many, the financial world can be bewildering. Yet financial planners do more than assist people in selecting the proper investments. Other activities can include cash management, cash budgeting, tax planning, investment review, goal setting, estate planning, determining insurance needs, projecting educational funding costs, and retirement planning. Financial planners help people over time, as well, to keep their money working for them and at the same time to keep them adequately prepared against risks.

If you are considering becoming a financial planner, you should investigate the regulatory requirements of your particular state regarding the distinction between a financial planner and an investment advisor representative. There is a gray area between these two occupations, and it is important to understand the lines drawn between them by your state. For instance, in most states, financial planners are not required to be licensed or registered, but investment advisors are. If you elect to go to work for a financial services company, they should be able to show you what licenses or registrations they maintain to allow them to conduct business and offer their various financial products and advice.

Becoming an effective financial planner requires a knowledge of many different but related subjects: all types of investments, such as stocks, bonds, and annuities; income, estate, and gift tax laws; estate planning and inheritance issues; alternative methods of savings; life and other forms of insurance and risk protection; financial statements and profit and loss statements; financial forecasts; the impact from the sale of a business; and alternate educational funding opportunities.

Some financial planners operate as sole practitioners and independent businesses, while others are affiliated with large financial services companies, such as IDS Financial Services, a division of American Express. Less than 10 percent achieve the designation of certified financial planner, which requires passing an examination that covers over 175 different topics. There are other designations planners can achieve, each with its own qualification and continuing education guidelines; these include *chartered financial consultant* (ChFC) and *personal financial specialist* (PFS).

Also, note that a financial planner is not the same as a financial analyst or a financial manager. Financial analysts produce economic forecasts in order for investors, lenders, and private equity firms to make investment decisions. They are traditionally found within large investment banks and companies, such as Merrill Lynch, UBS, JP Morgan, and Goldman Sachs. Financial managers are typically employed by a business or company to plan, direct, and coordinate accounting, investing, banking, insurance, securities, and other financial activities for their employer. Financial planners, on the other hand, usually consult with individuals on an hourly or other fee basis, but occasionally they earn additional income by participating in commissions earned through the sale of financial services products to their clients.

Ultimately, to be successful as a financial planner, you need to know all about finances and be meticulous with details, but you also need excellent people skills; offering good advice begins with patient listening to what a person needs.

BY THE NUMBERS

EMPLOYMENT LEVELS: According to the U.S. Bureau of Labor Statistics, there are 158,000 personal financial advisors/planners in the United States. This is separate and distinct from the number of financial analysts. The Consumer Federation of America estimates that, as of 2007, there were over 250,000 financial planners in the United States. (The large variation in these numbers results from the fact that titles within the financial world are so blurred.)

ACADEMIC REQUIREMENTS: There are no set academic requirements necessary to become a financial planner. However, it's essential to develop a thorough knowledge of all financial products and investment options. A college degree, one based in finance, is almost required, and many also choose to get an MBA in finance.

AVERAGE SALARY LEVELS: According to the U.S. Bureau of Labor Statistics, the median annual earnings for financial advisors/planners are **$62,700**. The average annual income range is **$41,860** to **$108,280**.

COLLEGE VS. REALITY

How would you compare the reality of your profession to the picture you had of it while in school?

My dad was an accountant, and he often spoke of clients asking for financial advice. I viewed accounting as too structured a career, so I did not follow in my dad's footsteps. In college, I had a picture only of what I did not want to be, not of what I wanted to be. I took a good mix of business, financial, and economics courses in school. The reality of being a financial planner is that until you build up a client base, you can starve to death. The older I get, the smarter my dad becomes; at least in accounting there is usually a steady stream of work out there, and if I had become an accountant, I could have gone on to specialize in financial planning.

—Financial planner, 5 years,
New Haven, Connecticut

Being an investment advisor or portfolio manager is not a profession that comes with an exact structure. It is not like being a dentist or a pharmacist. There is no one picture that fits this profession. The financial markets of the world are always changing, so the way you respond to them has to be adaptable to maximize the interest of your clients. There is no one way to do things in this business.

—Financial planner, 18 years,
St. Augustine, Florida

Much more of a relationship business — much more advising and planning and trusted advisor role than anticipated. Thought I would love picking stocks — which gets old. So I like the reality better.

—Investment advisor, 14 years,
Memphis, Tennessee

. . .

How would you rate your collegiate and graduate courses in preparing you for your profession on a scale of 1 to 10, with 10 being the best?

You can obtain a good understanding of the theories of economics and how financial markets are supposed to operate while in college, but you can't be taught how to balance these financial considerations with the personal needs of your clients. You may understand how stocks and bonds operate and what constitutes a perfect mix within those financial markets under certain economic conditions, but most of your clients' questions are being driven by personal needs and issues, not purely financial ones. Should I expand my business? Should I cash in on the hot real estate market? How will I pay for college for my three daughters? Can I really retire at fifty? You have to be a listener and a people person as well as have a sound understanding of everything financial. College cannot teach you all three.

—Registered investment advisor, 11 years,
Alpharetta, Georgia

I learned the economic theories and financial fundamentals, but what I didn't learn was how to get clients. If you try to go out on your own, unless your family or someone else stakes you until you can build up a client base, you can starve.

—**Financial advisor, 8 years,**
Frankfort, Kentucky

College gave me the basics. The real world teaches you the specifics. The key is to learn to balance the personal needs and wants of your clients with the harsh realities of the ever-changing financial markets. You have to think long-term and help your clients do the same. The pressures of life do not allow you or your clients to operate in a classroom setting. Partnerships dissolve, people die, people get cancer, and all those things cause people to reassess their financial goals. You have to think long-term and yet be constantly adaptable to changing circumstances. College does not teach you that.

—**Investment advisor, 13 years,**
Evansville, Indiana

THE BIGGEST SURPRISE

What most surprised you about your chosen profession?

The scope of the business and the industry. The business is much more diverse than I thought it would be. There is certainly more to people's financial lives than a twenty-two-year-old college student could realize.

—**Financial advisor, 5 years,**
Greensboro, North Carolina

The role you end up playing in people's lives. You anticipate that your contact with people will be more about the money you can make for them — and don't get me wrong, making money for your clients is at the center of being a financial or investment advisor — but clients are not as interested in the particulars of a certain stock or a new company as I thought they would be. They are running their own business so they can make the money that they want you to invest for them. What they are looking for is someone they can put their trust in. It is much more a relationship business than I anticipated.

—**Registered investment advisor, 17 years,**
Knoxville, Tennessee

How long it takes to establish your own client base. It takes more time than you will want, unless you have a lot of family connections right out of the gate.

—**Financial planner, 6 years,**
Roanoke, Virginia

HOURS AND ADVANCEMENT

How many hours do you work each week at your career?

Forty-five to fifty. It varies from week to week.

—**Financial planner, 10 years,**
Little Rock, Arkansas

If you consider all the studying of investment opportunities and keeping connected to the goings-on in the financial world, probably sixty a week.

—Registered investment advisor, 14 years,
University City, Missouri

Forty to forty-five in the office; ten to fifteen outside the office doing research and following trends.

—Financial planner, 9 years,
Wilmington, Delaware

. . .

Have you found advancement within your career easy or difficult?

Advancement means more clients.

—Financial planner, 6 years,
Clearwater, Florida

The first five years it was a grind building my client base. After that it picked up steadily. Good performance and word of mouth are the secrets.

—Financial planner, 10 years,
Tuscaloosa, Alabama

If your business is growing, you are continually advancing. I view advancement from two perspectives: how long my clients stay with me, and how many new clients they refer to me.

—Chartered financial consultant, 18 years,
Bellevue, Washington

THE BEST AND THE WORST

What do you spend most of your day doing? Describe a typical day.

My day usually starts at 6 AM, when I begin reading several different general and financial newspapers to get a sense of what is happening in the world. I am constantly monitoring the markets throughout the day as well as meeting with clients. My average client is around sixty-five, and I meet with each of them at least twice a year, unless circumstances dictate more frequent meetings. I try to take a midday break for a few hours for nourishment and exercise and then am back at studying and monitoring investment trends and being as actively involved in the markets as the needs of my clients dictate. My day ends around 9 PM, after I watch the last of several financial reports and shows on MSNBC and other networks.

—Registered investment advisor/portfolio
manager, 30 years, Nashville, Tennessee

Analyzing the financial world and looking for various economic trends that will provide opportunities for me to better serve my clients, and advising clients on a broad range of issues.

—Financial advisor, 12 years,
Bethesda, Maryland

Meetings with clients, studying and searching for new investment opportunities, making contacts that will help generate future clients, and keeping up with the changes in the financial markets and in the business and personal lives of my clients that could impact their financial goals.

—Registered investment advisor, 15 years, Oklahoma City, Oklahoma

. . .

What are the best parts of your profession?

Helping clients achieve their long-term goals.

—Financial advisor, 8 years, Albuquerque, New Mexico

The freedom this profession affords you to work in a business with almost unlimited income potential. It is up to you as to how much time you spend working.

—Registered investment advisor, 17 years, Lancaster, Pennsylvania

The personal relationships that I have made with my clients. Most start out as clients but end up as personal friends.

—Financial planner, 20 years, Brookfield, Wisconsin

. . .

What are the least enjoyable aspects of your profession?

When the idea that you just knew would produce some excellent income for your clients backfires.

—Registered investment advisor, 13 years, Arlington, Texas

Having to distinguish yourself from all the underqualified people holding themselves out to be financial planners, when really they are out to sell financial products or insurance products. Our industry is full of people who have severe conflicts of interest, but the public does not appreciate the situation. All the banks or large financial conglomerates are collecting fees at multiple levels that the public doesn't understand. The typical investment house setup has to pay the small-cap managers, the large-cap managers, the international fund managers, and so on. The public doesn't appreciate that they are paying all these different fees.

—Registered investment advisor, 19 years, Columbia, South Carolina

Losing your clients' money because of financial decisions you pursued that did not pan out as intended.

—Financial advisor, 7 years, Youngstown, Ohio

CHANGES IN THE PROFESSION

What changes do you foresee for your profession?

More *regulation*! A continued effort to rid the financial industry of questionable practices and questionable products.

—**Financial advisor, 12 years,**
Omaha, Nebraska

More of what has been gradually occurring over the past decade and a half, where the person the average customer deals with (whether it is at a bank or a brokerage house or an investment bank) is merely a relationship manager. He is not the one making the financial decisions with the customers' monies. He is simply the "face" for the company.

—**Registered investment advisor, 21 years,**
Boulder, Colorado

More commoditization of the activities of the investment advisors. More computer models making the decisions and more uniformity in the delivery of financial services as banks, investments houses, and insurance companies all try to offer one-stop shopping for all the needs of the customer.

—**Registered investment advisor, 15 years,**
Jackson, Mississippi

WOULD YOU DO IT
ALL OVER AGAIN?

Do you find your daily job fulfilling?

I don't have other professions to compare it to, but all in all financial planning offers one a nice mix of intellectual

challenge, entrepreneurialism, people interaction, and income potential.

—**Financial planner, 8 years,**
Providence, Rhode Island

I was in straight life insurance for several years before I became certified as a chartered financial consultant. My role as a financial consultant allows me to build longer-lasting relationships and help clients achieve specific goals, rather than spending so much time selling product.

—**Chartered financial consultant, 14 years,**
Louisville, Kentucky

I do now. I did not anticipate becoming a financial planner. Rather, my goal was to become an investment banker. I stayed in the traditional investment house setting for many years before going to work for myself as an investment advisor. My business life is still centered around the financial markets, but the way I relate to my clients is much less stressful and not as focused on the quantity of transactions.

—**Registered investment advisor, 18 years,**
Tigard, Oregon

. . .

Would you choose the same profession again?

I don't think so. I would go into the law or accounting. The public is confused about what a financial planner really does or is legally allowed to do, and it causes uncertainty as to my role in the business and financial world, which in turn leads to false expectations. The financial industry is mainly to blame because the labels that are assigned to individuals dealing with the public are not clearly defined. At my local bank the tellers now hand out business cards that say "Financial Representative." Many of these are kids who took no business or financial courses and could not tell you what a price-earnings ratio was if their life depended on it.

**—Registered investment advisor, 16 years,
Savannah, Georgia**

Yes, but I would try to get into the port-folio management side of the business earlier and away from the transactional side. Your outlook is less driven by commission-based transactions and more driven by long-term performance.

**—Registered investment advisor, 12 years,
Phoenix, Arizona**

Yes. This is a business where you can make a very good living and at the same time create some very great relation-ships that you will keep for a lifetime.

**—Financial planner, 22 years,
Cambridge, Massachusetts**

A CAREER IN

Education

SO YOU WANT TO BE A TEACHER

There are many parts of my career that make my job worthwhile. The best part is knowing that I am making a difference in a lot of lives. I am incredibly lucky because my job allows me to have immediate indicators that I am actually doing things well. There is nothing more gratifying than those "lightbulb" moments that occur in my class.

As everyone likes to say, educating our youth is one of the most important issues facing us as a society. State and local legislatures would seem to back that up, since most states and cities spend over half of their entire budget on public education at the elementary and secondary level. Yet if you ask the National Education Association (NEA), the teaching profession is in crisis.

The NEA, with 3.2 million members, is the largest organization of professional employees in the United States. It comprises elementary and secondary teachers, higher-education faculty, school administrators, retired teachers, and students preparing to become teachers. The crisis the NEA sees is the historic turnover that is looming in the teaching

115

profession. With a growing national population, student enrollments are rising rapidly. Yet more than a million teachers are nearing retirement. Education experts predict that between 2007 and 2017 the United States will need more than 2 million new teachers.

The national turnover rate for teachers is startling, especially when one considers how much work and study it takes to become a teacher. According to the NEA, approximately 20 percent of newly hired teachers leave the classroom within three years. In urban school districts, the rate is even higher, with almost 50 percent of teachers abandoning the profession within five years. The major culprit appears to be low pay, with starting salaries for teachers being considerably less than starting salaries in other professions. According to feedback from first-year teachers, many also feel overwhelmed by the expectations and scope of their job. Not all school districts have the resources for teacher mentoring programs, and so most first-year teachers are assigned the same tasks as veteran educators.

As a nation we are faced with a conundrum. If statistical trends continue, we will need an average of 200,000 new teachers each year for at least the next decade. Yet, according to the U.S. Department of Education's Institute of Education Statistics, in 2003–2004, only 106,000 of the 1.4 million bachelor's degrees in the United States were in the field of education.

If you are considering becoming a teacher, the conundrum continues. Once you complete your education and state certifications, it seems almost assured that you will be hired, but you know going in that salaries are low and expectations are high. According to the NEA, the national average starting salary for teachers in 2007 was $31,408, which is over $9,000 less than the average starting salary for a management trainee and over $13,000 less than for a registered nurse. Then there are the challenges of the classroom. A beginning teacher must not only negotiate the personalities, needs, and abilities of as many as thirty-five children but also deal with the needs and desires of their parents. A teacher must both stimulate and inspire each individual student and respond to the emails, phone calls, and concerns of parents.

One of the reasons for the gap between the public's vocal support for education and the lack of funding for teacher salaries is that certain myths persist about the teaching profession. Most think that teachers work only six hours a day and nine months a year. Yet, while teachers may only be at school six or seven hours a day, the reality is that teachers take a lot of work home. This includes creating lesson plans, grading papers, conducting parent-teacher conferences, responding to parents, attending meetings, and advising various student clubs and groups. Any teacher will tell you that the day is not over when the dismissal bell rings. A fifty-hour week is more often the norm than the exception.

Another myth is that, like their students, teachers have the summer off. This may be true for some, but many teachers use the summer break to take classes for certification renewal or to advance their careers. Over half of U.S. teachers have a master's degree, thus allowing them to be more knowledgeable and better teachers. Also, many teachers need to work summer jobs to help make up for their low base salaries.

An additional myth is that there is wasteful spending on school supplies. With over half of a city's annual budget spent on education, one would think that every student would have the books and supplies they need, but this isn't so. As those with a child in public school know, schools are constantly holding fund-raisers to buy necessary school supplies. In fact, according to the NEA, U.S. teachers spend an average of $443 a year out of their own pockets on materials for their classrooms and students.

With low pay, high expectations (particularly from parents), and strained budgets, just why would anyone want to become a teacher?

There is something magical about the process of learning. Shakespeare said that "knowledge is the wing wherewith we fly to heaven." Most of us remember teachers who inspired us and changed our lives.

For successful, long-lasting teachers, the desire to do that for children — to help students discover, grow, and achieve their full potential — typically must outweigh concerns over earning a high income. Indeed, this will probably have to remain the case, or else the national crisis over the shrinking number of teachers will only get worse.

BY THE NUMBERS

EMPLOYMENT LEVELS: According to data from the 2000 U.S. Census, there are 6.2 million teachers (of all levels) in the United States, and 71 percent are women. Of these, 3.1 million are elementary and middle school teachers, and 772,000 are secondary school teachers.

ACADEMIC REQUIREMENTS: Every state requires public school teachers to be licensed; licensure is not always required for teachers in private schools. License requirements differ from state to state, but all states require general-education teachers to have a bachelor's degree and to have completed an approved teacher training program, including supervised practice teaching. To ease the growing national teacher shortage, some states offer alternative licensing programs for teachers who hold a bachelor's degree in the subject they will be teaching but lack the necessary education courses.

AVERAGE SALARY LEVELS: According to the U.S. Bureau of Labor Statistics, the annual earnings for kindergarten and elementary, middle, and secondary school teachers range from a low of **$26,730** to a high of **$71,370**, with a median national annual earnings of **$41,400**.

COLLEGE VS. REALITY

How would you compare the reality of your profession to the picture you had of it while in school?

Until you enter your teaching career, you are too lost in your own idealism of changing lives — too much of a "Goodbye, Mr. Chips" expectation. Even student teaching is not fully realistic, as you don't have to handle all the paperwork, the parents, the emails, and the meetings.

—Elementary school teacher, 3 years, Wichita, Kansas

The basic mission of teaching that I envisioned while in school is the same — helping each individual student reach his or her potential. The process in achieving that goal has changed, with more emphasis on testing and endless assessments. We are not allowed the time to have a child connect with his or her subject out of true interest.

—Middle school teacher, 14 years, Lexington, Kentucky

My vision of teaching in school was overly idealistic. It was centered around communication and stimulation. It lacked the components of pre-class preparation, meetings with other teachers, and the interference (even if well intentioned) by the parents.

—Elementary school teacher, 8 years, Austin, Texas

. . .

How would you rate your collegiate and graduate courses in preparing you for your profession on a scale of 1 to 10, with 10 being the best?

6. Working with lesson planning and class structure and how to convey concepts doesn't work well without those who are the targets of the lessons — like teaching surgery with no body.

—Secondary school teacher, 10 years, Salem, Indiana

For an education major, unlike for some other majors, the course curriculum is well designed to prepare you for elementary education. The best preparation, however, was my student teaching.

—Elementary school teacher, 5 years, Charleston, West Virginia

I would rate it a 7. It could have been a 9 if it had incorporated more in-classroom involvement. There should be a longer practicum, or even possibly a staged one. That way those studying to become teachers could see real day-to-day operations before they finish their college courses. It would help weed out before graduation those individuals who end up feeling that teaching is not what they anticipated once they have their own classrooms.

—Middle school teacher, 7 years, Cedar Rapids, Iowa

THE BIGGEST SURPRISE

What most surprised you about your chosen profession?

The intense satisfaction of lecturing to a class and interacting with my students.

—Adjunct college professor, 6 years,
Memphis, Tennessee

The number of interruptions on a daily basis. If they hired me to be a teacher — let me teach! Leave the shuffling of paperwork and answering of emails from the office or the principal until the end of the day, or better yet once or twice a week.

—Elementary school teacher, 4 years,
Pensacola, Florida

The amount of planning that it takes to be an effective teacher. There is the planning in the morning before class, and then again the planning in the afternoon and evening after class.

—Middle school teacher, 12 years,
Kalamazoo, Michigan

HOURS AND ADVANCEMENT

How many hours do you work each week at your career?

Fifty to fifty-five hours per week.

—Secondary school teacher, 9 years,
Atlanta, Georgia

In the classroom, 8 AM to 3:30 PM. At home, one to two hours every evening, two to three hours on the weekend.

—Elementary school teacher, 11 years,
Indianapolis, Indiana

Forty at school per week — ten to twelve more at home per week

—Community college professor, 15 years,
Lexington, Kentucky

. . .

Have you found advancement within your career easy or difficult?

Difficult, because you have to have advanced degrees.

—Middle school teacher, 8 years,
Milwaukee, Wisconsin

Unlike most careers, teaching does not include the normal channels for advancement, unless you consider administration as advancement.

—Elementary school teacher, 12 years,
Jacksonville, Florida

We are not in sales. There are no bonuses, and many school districts have salary caps after so many years of service. If you are looking for constant advancement, choose another profession.

—Elementary school teacher, 18 years,
Knoxville, Tennessee

THE BEST AND THE WORST

What do you spend most of your day doing? Describe a typical day.

My day consists of supervising, teaching, being a taskmaster, planning lessons, and having to be very flexible.

—Middle school teacher, 6 years,
Sacramento, California

My day comprises lesson planning and attempting my best to fully implement my plans and complete all my daily subjects, while at the same time having to respond to emails from colleagues, the principal, and parents. Then after class or in the evening, evaluating a child's performance, before the entire process is repeated the next day.

—Elementary school teacher, 11 years,
Portland, Oregon

I review my plans for the day before I arrive at school; I then try my best to follow my plans within an environment of many interruptions. After class I usually have some type of meeting or activity with my fellow teachers or the students. In the evenings I usually grade papers or tests and look over my plans for the next day. A very long and exhausting day.

—Secondary school teacher, 8 years,
Fairfax, Virginia

. . .

What are the best parts of your profession?

There are many parts of my career that make my job worthwhile. The best part is knowing that I am making a difference in a lot of lives. I am incredibly lucky because my job allows me to have immediate indicators that I am actually doing things well. There is nothing more gratifying than those "lightbulb" moments that occur in my class.

—Elementary school teacher, 4 years,
Brentwood, Tennessee

Each day the students bring a new surprise to class through their questions, viewpoints, and comments.

—Middle school teacher, 16 years,
Annapolis, Maryland

Students who love to learn.

—Elementary school teacher, 21 years,
Boulder, Colorado

. . .

What are the least enjoyable aspects of your profession?

The committee meetings, department politics, and other aspects of teaching that are not directly related to your class.

—College professor, 5 years,
Chattanooga, Tennessee

121

The lack of support from supervisors, and the lack of community respect for teachers. No one wants to face the true cost of education. Teachers should be valued as a treasured resource and paid accordingly.

—**Elementary school teacher, 7 years,**
Boise, Idaho

The paperwork, which just keeps getting worse thanks to No Child Left Behind, and the parents who expect teachers to do their job of parenting for them.

—**Elementary school teacher, 5 years,**
Topeka, Kansas

CHANGES IN THE PROFESSION

What changes do you foresee for your profession?

More online courses and less of a personal connection with the students.

—**Community college professor, 17 years,**
Birmingham, Alabama

Increased use of technology and the elimination of more teaching assistant positions as school districts battle over budget demands versus property tax increases.

—**Secondary school teacher, 18 years,**
Garden City, New York

An obsession with testing, and all the paperwork that it will create for the teachers, as the school districts attempt to respond to No Child Left Behind and its endless changing of goals in search of exactly what is attainable and what is not.

—**Elementary school teacher, 5 years,**
Albuquerque, New Mexico

WOULD YOU DO IT ALL OVER AGAIN?

Do you find your daily job fulfilling?

Yes, because at the end of the year I see students who were lost and lacked self-esteem leave knowing they can learn. I am changing lives every day.

—**Elementary school teacher, 10 years,**
Columbus, Ohio

Yes. I feel I am contributing to something bigger than myself.

—**Middle school teacher, 13 years,**
Little Rock, Arkansas

In a broad sense, on a philosophical level. Yet each summer I have to force myself to go back to teaching because the pay is so low. I have a family, too, and at some level I think I am being unfair to my own children so that I can feel good about helping other people's children.

—**Elementary school teacher, 11 years,**
Monroe, Louisiana

. . .

Would you choose the same profession again?

Yes. Teaching is a passion for me. I know I am molding young lives.

—**Elementary school teacher, 9 years,**
Oxford, Mississippi

I would continue my education until I could get into teaching at the college level. The endless debates with parents caused me to leave a profession I loved.

I miss the students and my involvement with them, but the constant demands by parents simply became too much.

—**Elementary school teacher, 8 years,**
Tampa, Florida

Yes. The good outweighs the bad. My love for the students, whom I know I am helping, has been enough to overcome the parents who always know best, the increased paperwork, and the constant budgetary constraints.

—**Middle school teacher, 18 years,**
Riverside, California

CAREERS IN

The Social Sciences

SO YOU WANT TO BE A PSYCHOLOGIST

I expected to find more definitive answers to questions regarding human behavior, but I discovered that psychology as a science is a relatively recent phenomenon. Our understanding of human behavior is much further behind than the picture painted by the more mainstream "pop" psychologists. I was also shocked by the paucity of research supporting various treatments used by clinical psychologists, particularly in terms of the better-known psychodynamic treatment modalities. I have developed a great disdain for "professionals" who use untested methods and broad, hypothetical "theories" to guide their treatment approach.

Psychology is the study of the relationship between the human mind and human behavior, sometimes referred to as the science of human nature. More particularly, psychologists observe and investigate the physical, cognitive, emotional, and social aspects of human behavior. Psychology was considered a branch of philosophy until the middle of the nineteenth century, when a scientific form and later an experimental form of the discipline emerged in Germany.

For most people, the image of the psychologist is indelibly linked with Sigmund Freud. However, the history of psychology as a scholarly study dates back in Europe to the Middle Ages, and really the discipline goes back to the ancient Greeks. The word "psychology" takes its roots from the Greek, *psyche*, which was the term used by ancient philosophers like Plato and Aristotle in their elaborate theories about the mind.

The practice of psychology emerged in the United States in the late 1800s. William James published *Principles of Psychology* in 1890, and the first psychology clinic was established in Pennsylvania later that same decade. In the twentieth century, behaviorism, which limited psychological behavior to overt behavior that could be quantified and measured, was popularized by B. F. Skinner. Today, psychology follows an approach known as cognitive science, which is the interdisciplinary study of mind and intelligence, embracing philosophy, psychology, artificial intelligence, neuroscience, linguistics, and anthropology. Cognitive science emerged in the mid-1950s as researchers developed theories of mind based on complex representations and computational procedures, and in the mid-1970s the Cognitive Science Society was formed and the journal *Cognitive Science* began. Since then, more than sixty universities in North America, Europe, Asia, and Australia have established cognitive science programs.

Psychologists work in a variety of settings and go by many titles: *educational psychologists*, *industrial psychologists*, *developmental psychologists*, *social psychologists*, *experimental psychologists*, and more. As the titles imply, some specialize in research, while others work in hospitals, clinics, and schools to provide mental health–care services. Psychologists are also employed in specific applied areas such as industry, government, and nonprofit organizations, providing training, conducting research, and designing systems.

However, the largest specialty by far is *clinical psychology*, in which practicing psychologists work in counseling centers, in independent or group practices, or in association with hospitals or clinics. Clinical psychologists help mentally and emotionally disturbed clients adjust to life issues. They also interview patients and give diagnostic tests. Psychotherapy and behavior modification programs can be provided by clinical psychologists in individual, family, or group sessions. Clinical psychologists also collaborate with physicians and other specialists to develop and implement the best treatment for the individual patient.

A doctoral degree is required to become a licensed clinical psychologist, which means five to seven years of postgraduate education. Most prospective psychologists spend two years in a master's program, four or more years in a doctoral program (plus more time completing a dissertation), and one year in an internship. Courses in statistical and quantitative research methods are key components of any graduate program in psychology. For anyone wanting to become a psychologist, a good background in the social, physical, and biological sciences is quite helpful, along with a foundation in psychology, statistics, and math.

Although the different titles may be confusing, there are distinctions between *clinical psychologists* (for whom a PhD is required) and *licensed professional counselors* and *clinical social workers* (for both of whom a master's is traditionally required), and between these and *psychiatrists* (who attend medical school and specialize in psychiatry). One of the most important distinctions is that psychologists, with few exceptions, are not permitted to write prescriptions for their patients, while psychiatrists are.

BY THE NUMBERS

EMPLOYMENT LEVELS: According to the U.S. Bureau of Labor Statistics, there are approximately 179,000 psychologists. One out of four works within or is affiliated with an educational institution in a position other than counseling, and four out of ten are self-employed.

ACADEMIC REQUIREMENTS: A doctoral degree is usually required for employment as an independent licensed clinical or counseling psychologist; graduate study, including a dissertation, typically takes five to seven years to complete. Psychologists in independent practice or who offer patient care are required to be licensed by the state in which they are practicing; licensing requirements, including the number of years of supervised experience, vary by state and the nature of the practice, but all licensed psychologists must pass the National Psychology Licensing Exam, administered by the Association of State and Provincial Boards of Psychology.

AVERAGE SALARY LEVELS: According to the U.S. Bureau of Labor Statistics, the median annual earnings of both wage and salaried clinical, counseling, and school psychologists are **$59,950**; on average, salaries range from **$32,280** to **$92,250**.

COLLEGE VS. REALITY

How would you compare the reality of your profession to the picture you had of it while in school?

As regards the general environment in which I would practice, I think I had a relatively accurate picture of what that would be like. What I did not fully understand was how emotionally draining the practice would be.

—Clinical psychologist, 7 years,
Fort Wayne, Indiana

The major distinction for me between what I anticipated while in school and what I have found in actual practice is a lack of clarity that what I am doing will have the desired results for the people I treat. As a student I felt that progress in actual cases would be more clearly definable, and unfortunately that is not the case.

—Clinical psychologist, 4 years,
Grand Rapids, Michigan

How I envisioned my practice while in school and how it has unfolded have differed in large part because of my experiences both inside and outside my practice. While in school I anticipated a practice that would be focused on adults who were trying to best cope with life's crises. However, once I had the opportunity to work with children, I realized that I could have a much greater impact on the lives of others if I focused on children and adolescents. It took actual sessions with all different groups for me to come to fully appreciate this reality.

—Clinical psychologist, 11 years,
New Rochelle, New York

. . .

How would you rate your collegiate and graduate courses in preparing you for your profession on a scale of 1 to 10, with 10 being the best?

My undergraduate courses did not really prepare me for the real world but rather prepared me for my graduate studies. As I progressed through my master's and then doctoral program, I felt more prepared for what I now face, but it was my internship that I value as the best real-world training.

—Educational psychologist, 5 years,
Manchester, New Hampshire

By the time I completed my dissertation and one year of postdoctoral work, I finally felt prepared to practice psychology. Yet even with all this schooling (eleven years), I quickly learned how little we really know about the human mind.

—Developmental psychologist, 3 years,
Durham, North Carolina

From an academic perspective, I feel that my years and years of education prepared me rather well for my profession, equipping me with skills in research design and statistical interpretation. However, I wish there had been some additional focus on the business side of the practice of psychology and providing treatment within the structure of insurance and managed care.

—Clinical psychologist, 6 years,
Mansfield, Ohio

THE BIGGEST SURPRISE

What most surprised you about your chosen profession?

I expected to find more definitive answers to questions regarding human behavior, but I discovered that psychology as a science is a relatively recent phenomenon. Our understanding of human behavior is much further behind than the picture painted by the more mainstream "pop" psychologists. I was also shocked by the paucity of research supporting various treatments used by clinical psychologists, particularly in terms of the better-known psychodynamic treatment modalities. I have developed a great disdain for "professionals" who use untested methods and broad, hypothetical "theories" to guide their treatment approach.

—Pediatric clinical psychologist, 2 years,
Wilmington, Delaware

That there are lots of people who get into this field because they have a broad notion of wanting to help someone, yet their own individual lives are anything but stable. I am fearful that these practitioners have the potential of doing more harm than good.

—Clinical psychologist, 14 years,
Brandon, Florida

How connected I would become to my patients. The concept of professional detachment is a good academic model, but the children I work with stay with me in my thoughts long after they have completed their sessions.

—Clinical psychologist, 8 years,
Augusta, Georgia

HOURS AND ADVANCEMENT

How many hours do you work each week at your career?

Thirty-five to forty.

—Experimental psychologist, 11 years,
Somerville, Massachusetts

Ten to fifteen per week. Being a psychologist and part of a private group practice allows me raise my children and still work ten to fifteen hours per week.

—Clinical psychologist, 6 years,
Annapolis, Maryland

Forty to forty-five.

—Educational psychologist, 17 years,
Athens, Georgia

...

Have you found advancement within your career easy or difficult?

Just to attain the position of a licensed psychologist requires a series of advancements that are predicated on long hours and dedication to your goal. Once you finally reach your goal, advancement can be defined so many different ways. Working on a research project that can have a major impact in treating others could be deemed a more advanced step than a private practitioner building his or her practice from more and more referrals, depending on what one's goals are.

—Social psychologist, 9 years,
Englewood, Colorado

Advancement can mean going into management if you work in a school, hospital, government agency, or even industrial setting. In private practice it can mean a growing practice, more clinical sessions, or greater income. Do any of those constitute advancement? It depends on whom you ask.

—Developmental psychologist, 16 years,
Cherry Hill, Pennsylvania

For me, advancement meant the opportunity to teach part-time. It gave me a break from the emotional aspects associated with clinical work and refreshed my spirit and love for the work.

—Educational psychologist, 15 years,
Dallas, Texas

THE BEST AND THE WORST

What do you spend most of your day doing? Describe a typical day.

In my private practice, my days are made up of a mix of clinical work, evaluations, testing, and writing. The exact mix and focus of these different activities are dictated by the needs of my patients.

—Clinical psychologist, 9 years,
Gainesville, Florida

My days are centered primarily around clinical sessions with different patients referred to me within the hospital community where I am employed. At the same time I am able to still participate in some ongoing research projects with which the hospital is participating.

—Clinical psychologist, 11 years,
Tacoma, Washington

My days as an industrial psychologist can be varied but usually include some mixture of or participation in consulting with various business clients on workplace culture, work productivity, or improving the managerial process of interviewing new employees.

—Industrial psychologist, 21 years,
Arlington, Virginia

. . .

What are the best parts of your profession?

As a practicing psychologist I am able to have an intimate relationship with my patients, and yet it is within a structure that has a defined beginning and a defined ending, so I know going in that it will not be permanent. This allows me to give my best efforts with each patient and yet know all along that I must move on to the next one.

—Clinical psychologist, 10 years,
Brentwood, Tennessee

A doctorate in psychology opens up so many different options. You can apply your knowledge to a career path devoted solely to empirical research if that best fits your personality and goals. You can work in a school setting or in a hospital setting. You can become an industrial psychologist, or you can set up your own clinical practice.

—Social psychologist, 14 years,
Newark, New Jersey

Seeing my patients improve, so that the daily lives of families are more stable.

—Clinical psychologist, 7 years,
San Bernardino, California

. . .

What are the least enjoyable aspects of your profession?

The emotional drain that comes with the job. It is a real balancing act to maintain your own well-structured family life while at the same time counseling people whose lives are coming unglued.

—Clinical psychologist, 12 years,
Dublin, Ohio

The inability to follow up with my young patients and see how their lives are turning out.

—Pediatric clinical psychologist, 5 years,
Charleston, South Carolina

The misconception that many people have of psychologists and what we can effectively accomplish. Shows like *Dr. Phil* do a disservice to the profession. Dr. Phil follows a treatment philosophy known as cognitive behavior therapy, which is based on the idea that our thoughts, not external things, like people, situations, and events, cause our feelings and behaviors. The benefit of this fact is that we can change the way we think to feel/act better even if the situation does not change. Dr. Phil twists it to fit a ten- to fifteen-minute format. Most people don't know this. A normal treatment sequence of this style of therapy averages between fifty and one hundred hours of sessions!

—Clinical psychologist, 18 years,
Milwaukee, Wisconsin

CHANGES IN THE PROFESSION

What changes do you foresee for your profession?

The insurance companies will continue to have a larger role in determining the level of services that psychologists can offer to their patients.

—Clinical psychologist, 14 years,
Mesa, Arizona

There will continue to be a major push by psychologists for the legal authority to write medical prescriptions, but this is a very slippery slope for our profession to go down.

—Clinical psychologist, 9 years,
Des Plaines, Illinois

Managed care will continue to dominate the way our services are delivered to the general public. I also see national health care around the corner, and I am concerned how the mental health field will be affected when that does occur. It could either be very bad, in that mental health issues will be pushed to the back of the bus, or it could be an improvement, if the national coverage places mental health services on a par with other medical issues.

—Educational psychologist, 22 years,
Portland, Oregon

WOULD YOU DO IT ALL OVER AGAIN?

Do you find your daily job fulfilling?

Yes. It is very rewarding to assist someone to cope with life on more manageable terms.

—Clinical psychologist, 11 years,
Wilmington, North Carolina

Fulfillment in life is a moving target for most people. What fulfills them in their twenties may not fulfill them in their forties. I think that I am contributing to the betterment of society one person at a time.

—Educational psychologist, 19 years,
Jacksonville, Florida

It find it both rewarding and emotionally draining. I have yet to decide if that combination equates with fulfilling. Ask me in five more years.

—Clinical psychologist, 5 years,
St. Charles, Missouri

. . .

Would you choose the same profession again?

I wanted to do something in the healthcare field. Dentistry was out — I mean, really, putting my hands in people's mouths all day. Surgery seemed intriguing, but I was much more interested in the mental side of health than in the physical side. And I loved doing research. So psychology was a good fit for me.

—Experimental psychologist, 15 years,
Aurora, Illinois

Not exactly. I would have instead gone to medical school and become a psychiatrist, as I believe the medical school training would have benefited both me and ultimately my patients, and I would be able to write prescriptions as I deemed them necessary for my own patients.

—Clinical psychologist, 12 years,
Louisville, Kentucky

Yes. It allows me to work part-time helping families while still being able to have and enjoy my own.

—Clinical psychologist, 8 years,
Little Rock, Arkansas

SO YOU WANT TO BE A
SPEECH PATHOLOGIST

I was drawn to deaf people even as a young child. I wanted to understand why they did not hear and speak like we did. I have a passion for helping hearing-impaired and speech-impaired children integrate into society so they can experience as normal a childhood as possible. However, I think that the profession should be more specialized. A speech pathologist can be called upon to deal with patients whose communication difficulties can stem from a broad range of symptoms, from speech disorders to hearing impairments to autism to stroke. At times you can feel overwhelmed by the sheer number of different conditions that you encounter from week to week.

For those who have problems with their speech, to live in an age of communication is a blessing and a challenge. While there have never been more ways to communicate without speech, there are also many more contexts in which not being able to speak, or speak clearly, causes difficulties. Speech pathologists are the key to improving the lives of the millions of people around the world who live with such limitations.

Speech pathologists are formally referred to in the occupational directories as *speech-language pathologists* and are also sometimes called *speech therapists*. As professionals they assess, diagnose, treat, and help to prevent speech, language, cognitive-communication, voice, swallowing, fluency, and other related disorders. *Audiologists*, who work with hearing, balance, and ear-related problems, are a closely associated profession. In fact, both professions are combined into one national professional organization, the American Speech-Language-Hearing Association (ASHA), which has over 127,000 members.

Speech-language pathologists work with people who cannot produce speech sounds or cannot produce them clearly; those with speech rhythm and fluency problems, such as stuttering; people with voice disorders, such as inappropriate pitch or harsh voice; those with problems understanding and producing language; those who wish to improve their communication skills by modifying an accent; and those with cognitive communication impairments, such as attention, memory, and problem-solving disorders. They also work with people who have swallowing difficulties.

As a separate profession in the United States, speech pathology dates back to 1925. Over the next two decades the academic, scientific, and practice seeds of the profession were planted. Between 1945 and 1965, many assessment and therapy approaches were developed to improve the psychological processing underlying communication disorders. For the next decade, the profession viewed language disorders as linguistic in nature, and they were treated separately from speech disorders. Beginning in the mid-1970s, this approach was reconsidered and reframed, and today the profession of speech pathology combines communicative, linguistic, cultural, and everyday-life contexts.

Speech, language, and swallowing difficulties can result from a variety of causes, including stroke, brain injury or deterioration, developmental delays or disorders, learning disabilities, cerebral palsy, cleft palate, voice pathology, mental retardation, hearing loss, or emotional problems. Problems can be congenital, developmental, or acquired. Speech pathologists use qualitative and quantitative assessment methods, including standardized tests, as well as special instruments, to analyze and diagnose the nature and extent of speech, language, and swallowing impairments.

Speech pathologists tailor their care to each patient's needs. For individuals with little or no speech capability, speech pathologists may select augmentative or alternative communication methods, including automated devices and sign language. They teach these individuals how to make sounds, improve their voices, or increase their oral or written language skills to communicate more effectively. They also teach individuals how to strengthen muscles or use compensatory strategies to swallow without choking or inhaling food or liquid.

All fifty states require a master's degree or equivalent to practice speech pathology. In addition, forty-seven states require speech pathologists to be licensed if they work in a health-care environment; to be licensed, they must pass a national examination and complete several hundred hours of clinical experience. The American Speech-Language-Hearing Association developed and commissions a national examination administered in conjunction with the Praxis series of exams, relied upon by states for certification and licensures, for graduate-level speech therapists who want to become licensed speech-language pathologists. However, only a dozen or so states require the same license for one to practice in a public school setting, and they allow speech pathologists to practice after being issued a teaching certificate if the teacher has a master's degree in speech pathology. Over two hundred U.S. colleges and universities offer graduate programs in speech pathology, with courses in anatomy, physiology, acoustics, and the psychological aspects of communication. Graduate students also receive clinical training in communication disorders.

As the overall U.S. population ages and the baby-boomer generation retires, there is a concurrent rise in medical conditions such as stroke and hearing loss. Medical advances are also improving the survival rate for trauma and stroke victims. Both of these trends will improve the opportunities for careers in speech pathology. Additionally, employment of speech pathologists in educational services will increase with growing elementary and secondary school enrollments, and due to the fact that federal law guarantees special education and related services to all eligible children with disabilities.

BY THE NUMBERS

EMPLOYMENT LEVELS: According to the U.S. Bureau of Labor Statistics, there are approximately 96,000 speech pathologists. The American Speech-Language-Hearing Association lists over 127,000 members, but this total includes pathologists, audiologists, and speech, language, and hearing scientists.

ACADEMIC REQUIREMENTS: All states require a master's degree or equivalent to practice speech pathology. In addition, forty-seven states require speech pathologists to be licensed, which involves passing the Praxis series national examination on speech-language pathology and accumulating over three hundred hours of supervised clinical experience.

AVERAGE SALARY LEVELS: According to the U.S. Bureau of Labor Statistics, the annual median earnings for speech pathologists are **$52,410**; the overall average range is **$34,720** to **$82,420**. Traditionally, positions within school systems offer the lowest salaries.

COLLEGE VS. REALITY

How would you compare the reality of your profession to the picture you had of it while in school?

Based upon the clinical portion of my graduate courses, I had a relatively accurate view of what my role as a speech pathologist would entail.

—Speech pathologist, 5 years,
Burlington, Vermont

I had a good understanding of the physiological, anatomical, and acoustical aspects of my profession, but I was not prepared for the depth of the psychological aspects of an inability to effectively communicate.

—Speech pathologist, 3 years,
Montgomery, Alabama

College and graduate courses can give you a good overview, but there are so many different issues that a speech pathologist faces in a real-life practice that the transition from academia to a full-time clinical practice can be a little overwhelming.

—Speech pathologist, 2 years,
Baltimore, Maryland

...

How would you rate your collegiate and graduate courses in preparing you for your profession on a scale of 1 to 10, with 10 being the best?

Based on the combination of course material and clinical exposure, I would rank it an 8.

—Speech pathologist, 7 years,
Fort Smith, Arkansas

From the standpoint of the anatomical and acoustical fundamentals, I was prepared, but as for dealing with patients and their families, I was not.

—Speech pathologist/educator, 9 years,
Joplin, Missouri

What college did not prepare me for was the business side of setting up my own practice or becoming a member of a multidisciplinary practice that included psychologists and social workers. You are really in the dark as to this aspect of the profession.

—Clinical speech pathologist, 4 years,
Spring Hill, Tennessee

THE BIGGEST SURPRISE

What most surprised you about your chosen profession?

The vast distinction between income levels. A private practitioner can receive a gross income that is as much as double that of a speech pathologist in a school setting.

—Educator/speech pathologist, 11 years,
Decatur, Georgia

The difficulty in convincing a patient's parents of the importance of following your advice and working with their child so that the treatment options have a chance to have a positive effect.

—Clinical speech pathologist, 5 years,
Lawton, Oklahoma

How much individuals in our profession are in demand. With people living longer and surviving strokes, and all the front-line health-care organizations from hospitals to nursing homes to home-health companies, the need for speech pathologists seems to be growing and growing.

—Speech pathologist, 14 years,
Bloomfield, New Jersey

HOURS AND ADVANCEMENT

How many hours do you work each week at your career?

I work in a school environment, and my hours usually track those of the regular teaching staff — about thirty-five in-school hours.

—Educator/speech pathologist, 8 years,
Asheville, North Carolina

I work in a group practice that has psychologists, licensed professional counselors, and speech pathologists. I am able to set my workload around how many patients I want to see week to week, which in turn allows me to meet my own family obligations. It can vary from fifteen to twenty hours on the low side to twenty-five to thirty on the high side.

—Clinical speech pathologist, 16 years,
Lexington, Kentucky

I work in a hospital setting and have regular shifts that I meet. It averages out at thirty-eight to forty hours per week.

—Speech pathologist, 4 years,
Cincinnati, Ohio

. . .

Have you found advancement within your career easy or difficult?

Advancement within a school or classroom setting is very limited. You may gradually make more, but the income increases come in such small increments that they are usually absorbed by the rising costs of living.

—Educator/speech pathologist, 15 years,
Gladstone, Missouri

I work in a multidiscipline practice, so advancement is measured in more patients/clients and more gross billings. There is plenty of work out there if you want it.

—Clinical speech pathologist, 7 years,
Mount Pleasant, South Carolina

I view advancement based upon the number of referrals I receive from other patients or health-care providers. Within this context, advancement has come in an orderly fashion.

—Speech pathologist, 5 years,
Memphis, Tennessee

THE BEST AND THE WORST

What do you spend most of your day doing? Describe a typical day.

I work in an elementary school as a daily classroom instructor for children with hearing and speech problems.

—Educator/speech pathologist, 8 years,
Jacksonville, Florida

As a speech pathologist who works in a hospital setting, I spend my day with the patients to whom I am assigned. That can range from geriatric patients who have to relearn their speech patterns, to someone who has received brain injuries from an automobile accident that has impaired his or her ability to speak, to a patient who is having to adjust to the impact of surgery for a cochlear implant.

—Clinical speech pathologist, 13 years,
Rochester, New York

Each day is different in the context of the type of patient I am working with. As a speech pathologist employed in association with a large home-health agency, I travel to people's homes to assist them with all types of speech problems. The largest percentage of my current practice deals with accident victims who are out of the hospital but not ready to re-enter society, as well as stroke victims who need my assistance in regaining their ability to communicate.

—Speech pathologist, 5 years,
Modesto, California

. . .

What are the best parts of your profession?

Seeing children improve to the level that they are socially accepted by their peers.

—Speech pathologist/educator, 4 years,
Newport News, Virginia

The availability of abundant work. As a roving freelancer, you can work almost as much as you desire.

—Speech pathologist, 9 years,
Fort Lauderdale, Florida

Healing patients allows them to return to the norm of society as relates to their ability to communicate after a stroke, accident, or major injury.

—Clinical speech pathologist, 19 years,
El Paso, Texas

. . .

What are the least enjoyable aspects of your profession?

Having parents accept the limitations of their children and not be committed enough to work with them to ensure improvement.

—Speech pathologist, 11 years,
Olympia, Washington

The low pay if you work in a school environment.

—Speech pathologist, 3 years,
Baton Rouge, Louisiana

The emotional strain that can come from working with people who have physical impairments, and with their families, who do not have the background to appreciate what you are doing and how gradual improvement can be.

—Clinical speech pathologist, 7 years,
Warwick, Rhode Island

CHANGES IN THE PROFESSION

What changes do you foresee for your profession?

143

More emphasis on early identification of speech and language problems in younger and younger children.

—Speech pathologist, 10 years, Akron, Ohio

Improved survival rates for trauma and stroke patients, which in turn will create a need for more intervention and involvement by speech pathologists.

—Clinical speech pathologist, 17 years, Rochester, Minnesota

The development of new therapies and earlier and improved implants and amplification techniques and devices.

—Speech pathologist, 7 years, Lancaster, Pennsylvania

WOULD YOU DO IT ALL OVER AGAIN?

Do you find your daily job fulfilling?

Yes. It is very rewarding to help children with the most basic of issues — communicating with others.

—Speech pathologist/educator, 3 years, Las Cruces, New Mexico

I do. I knew early on that I wanted to work in a school environment with very young children with hearing and speech problems.

—Speech pathologist, 6 years, Elizabeth, New Jersey

It is more emotional than I anticipated. I work in a hospital setting, primarily with stroke and trauma survivors, and it can be both rewarding and draining at the same time. I am good at what I do, and I know I am making a difference in people's lives.

—Clinical speech pathologist, 12 years, Las Vegas, Nevada

. . .

Would you choose the same profession again?

Yes. I was drawn to deaf people even as a young child. I wanted to understand why they did not hear and speak like we did. I have a passion for helping hearing-impaired and speech-impaired children integrate into society so they can experience as normal a childhood as possible. However, I think that the profession should be more specialized. A speech pathologist can be called upon to deal with patients whose communication difficulties can stem from a broad range of symptoms, from speech disorders to hearing impairments to autism to stroke. At times you can feel overwhelmed by the sheer number of different conditions that you encounter from week to week.

—Speech pathologist/educator, 5 years, Jackson, Mississippi

I would most likely go into psychology instead. There are so many psychological aspects that are part of any speech impairment or deficiency, and it is that aspect of the patient puzzle that most intrigues me.

**—Clinical speech pathologist, 9 years,
Mobile, Alabama**

Yes. You will not get rich, but you can make an adequate living and help those in need.

**—Speech pathologist, 18 years,
Dearborn, Michigan**

SO YOU WANT TO BE A
SOCIAL WORKER OR CLINICAL THERAPIST

I was surprised to learn that I had chosen a career that was so emotionally draining that I faced burnout at thirty. Only by moving into a management role, and also doing some part-time teaching, grant work, and presentations to the community, was I able to offer myself a sufficient balance to remain in this career that I know is where I belong.

In the United States, the field of social work traces its roots back to the summer of 1898, when the first class titled "Social Work" was offered at Columbia University. From this singular academic beginning, the critical role of the social worker grew in our society. There are now over 400 Bachelor of Social Work programs offered at U.S. colleges and universities, and over 150 programs offer a master's degree in social work.

Social work is a profession devoted to helping people function the best they can in their environment. In broad strokes, this can mean providing direct social services to individuals, acting as therapists for clients, and working to improve social conditions.

The wide-ranging mission of social work owes much to the inspirational life of Jane Addams, who devoted her life to helping the poor. Born to a life of privilege in 1860, Addams completed Rockford Seminary and wanted to become a doctor, but her family all but forbade it. While traveling in Europe, she became inspired by Toynbee Hall, a settlement house (an institution providing community services in urban areas) in the slums of London. In 1889, after returning to the United States, she founded Hull House, one of the first settlement houses in the country. By 1893, with the country rocked by a depression, Hull House was serving over two thousand people a week, primarily immigrants, offering medical care, child care, and legal aid, as well as vocational classes and classes in English. Addams's energy was unstoppable; she was a founder of the Women's Peace Party, the International Congress of Women, the American Civil Liberties Union, and the NAACP, and she was the first vice president of the National American Woman Suffrage Association. In 1931, she received the Nobel Peace Prize.

The spirit of Jane Addams still permeates the profession of social work. Many of the benefits Americans take for granted resulted in great part from the persistent efforts of social workers — unemployment insurance, disability pay, worker's compensation, Social Security benefits, improved access to health care for the disabled and the elderly, and programs for the prevention of spousal and child abuse, as well as destigmatization of and help for treating mental illness.

If you're looking for a career in which you can make a difference in the daily lives of others, consider social work, but be aware that the hours can be long and stressful, and starting salaries can be lower than in many other professions. A bachelor's degree in social work is the most common minimum requirement to qualify for a position as a social worker. However, adding a master's degree in social work is becoming more common, as it increases your income potential and allows you to do clinical work, such as act as a therapist. In school, many people concentrate in sociology, but courses in psychology, political science, and economics are helpful as well. Almost every city of any size in the United

States has a social assistance agency, thus creating an opportunity for undergraduate and graduate students to have hands-on training in an agency setting. This gives students a chance to interact with individuals faced with real needs, such as a disability, a domestic conflict, substance abuse, unemployment, or inadequate housing.

As a career, social work provides a variety of employment opportunities and settings. Social workers are found in or affiliated with public agencies, hospitals, clinics, public school systems, nursing homes, police departments, courts, and private business, and they also act as private practitioners.

Many social workers elect to specialize, and their titles indicate their focus. *Child, family, and school social workers* provide services and assistance to families and children, particularly so children can succeed academically. *Medical and public health social workers* provide persons and families with the psychological support to cope with acute or chronic illness. Some participate in postdischarge planning, and some participate on interdisciplinary teams in the evaluation of certain patient groups. *Mental health and substance abuse social workers* participate in the assessment and treatment of individuals with mental illness or substance abuse problems. *Social work planners and policymakers* concentrate on the development of programs to address broad social issues, such as homelessness, poverty, child abuse, and violence, and they may participate in research and in legislative issues.

Most states require practicing social workers to be licensed, certified, or registered, although the specific policies vary somewhat from state to state. Most practicing social workers fall into the category of either *licensed clinical social worker* (LCSW) or *licensed professional counselor* (LCP). In the world of social work, the term "licensed clinical therapist" typically is an unofficial designation indicating someone who can act as a therapist to clients. Also, though a licensed social worker may act as therapist, this does not make that person the same as a trained psychologist, which requires a doctoral degree and other particular licensing and certification requirements.

BY THE NUMBERS

EMPLOYMENT LEVELS: According to the U.S. Bureau of Labor Statistics, there are 562,000 social workers in the United States. Child, family, and school social workers represent the largest category with 272,000, followed by mental health and substance abuse counselors with 116,000, and medical and public health social workers with 110,000.

ACADEMIC REQUIREMENTS: A bachelor's degree in social work is the most common minimum requirement for a job as a social worker. However, a master's in social work is required for one to act as a clinical therapist or a licensed professional counselor. There are 442 bachelor's, 168 master's, and 80 doctoral programs in social work offered in the United States. An accredited bachelor's program requires four hundred hours of supervised field experience, while a master's program requires nine hundred hours of supervised field experience.

AVERAGE SALARY LEVELS: According to the National Association of Social Workers, individuals with a bachelor's degree in social work should expect a starting salary of up to **$30,000** (depending on type of work, experience, and location), while those with a master's in social work can expect up to **$40,000**. Those with a doctoral degree in social work can anticipate a starting salary above **$40,000**. Experienced private practitioners and senior administrators can earn up to **$100,000** a year.

COLLEGE VS. REALITY

How would you compare the reality of your profession to the picture you had of it while in school?

A fairly accurate assessment all in all as to what you will be dealing with, with most of this resulting from the internships available to most people in this field throughout your academic phase, but not as to the intensity of the work.

—Licensed clinical social worker, 3 years, Warren, Michigan

For me, the reality was quite different from my idealistic assumptions. There is no substitute for sitting in the same room with real, live, flesh-and-blood human beings listening to them as they tell the story of their lives and problems, as contrasted with reading about a case study in a textbook. Nothing can adequately prepare one for the encounter except the actual encounter and experience itself. Before I entered my chosen profession I had only a vague notion and desire to want to help people. How that manifested and worked itself out was, for me, an indirect and rather accidental journey. Furthermore, traditional school environments — whether they be undergraduate or graduate — typically are not able to duplicate the reality of a community agency or organization. If a student is lucky, he or she might be able to do an internship or field placement; however, community agencies are often private, not-for-profit, small organizations with big missions and limited resources. This is now a highly regulated and "managed" business, and one does not necessarily have the freedom or autonomy that one might assume or want as compared to twenty years ago.

—Licensed professional counselor/mental health service provider, 34 years, Brownsville, Tennessee

By the time they graduate, most people who elect to study for a career in social counseling are not naïve about the environment in which they will be working, but the profession is more emotionally draining than one can ever picture in school.

—Licensed clinical social worker, 4 years, Roanoke, Virginia

. . .

How would you rate your collegiate and graduate courses in preparing you for your profession on a scale of 1 to 10, with 10 being the best?

Most college programs in social work allow you the opportunity to work in a nonprofit agency setting while in both undergraduate and graduate school, so by the time you enter private practice or agency practice, you have a good indication of what your day-to-day work will consist of. But when it arrived, it was more demanding than I anticipated.

—Licensed clinical social worker, 7 years, Lawrence, Kansas

I would give my undergraduate courses a 7. Besides providing the obvious course studies, they were effective in introducing me to the importance of research in this field.

—Social worker, 5 years, Anderson, Indiana

I would recommend a master's in clinical psychology or a master's in social work. Undergraduate school provides you with a foundation, but the concentrated focus in graduate school along with the readily available internships is the best way to be most prepared for this profession.

—**Licensed professional counselor, 12 years, Quincy, Massachusetts**

THE BIGGEST SURPRISE

What most surprised you about your chosen profession?

I was surprised to learn that I had chosen a career that was so emotionally draining that I faced burnout at thirty. Only by moving into a management role, and also doing some part-time teaching, grant work, and presentations to the community, was I able to offer myself a sufficient balance to remain in this career that I know is where I belong.

—**Licensed clinical social worker, 6 years, Nashville, Tennessee**

The lack of appreciation for mental disorders by the insurance industry as a whole.

—**Licensed clinical social worker, 5 years, East Point, Georgia**

The low pay for professionals who have such a direct impact on so many people's lives.

—**Social worker, 2 years, Little Rock, Arkansas**

HOURS AND ADVANCEMENT

How many hours do you work each week at your career?

Forty hours is a usual week for me, based upon my weekly load of clients.

—**Social worker, 8 years, Tallahassee, Florida**

I usually work fifty hours a week based upon a combination of my counseling duties and my supervisory duties.

—**Licensed professional counselor, 12 years, Allentown, Pennsylvania**

My weekly number of hours varies based upon how many client sessions I am willing to book. As a private practitioner, I am in control of just how busy I elect to be.

—**Licensed clinical social worker, 15 years, Kettering, Ohio**

. . .

Have you found advancement within your career easy or difficult?

By the nature of our profession, if you work in a public agency setting, advancement means moving into management and having less time to act in a clinical role.

—**Licensed clinical social worker, 9 years, Trenton, New Jersey**

For private practitioners, advancement is usually viewed as having more patients. For me it is about having more successful outcomes with the patients I do have.

—Licensed clinical social worker, 22 years,
Gary, Indiana

It depends on whether you want to focus on clinical work or managerial matters. If you want to remain devoted to seeing patients in a clinical setting, the only way to advance is to find an agency position in a larger city or move into private practice. If you desire to move into management, there are positions that would be deemed advancements, at least from an income perspective.

—Licensed professional counselor, 10 years,
Greenville, South Carolina

THE BEST AND THE WORST

What do you spend most of your day doing? Describe a typical day.

I am a manager, so I see clients, but I also supervise other clinicians, keep up with facility issues, do marketing, file complaints, etc. Yet at the same time I am held to productivity standards and am expected to spend 70 percent of my time in individual sessions with clients and 30 percent in administration, supervision, and general office operations. My position causes me to shift gears frequently from administrative to clinical work. For instance, I could be

seeing a client and have Joint Commission on Accreditation or Licensure auditors show up at the same time. I could be seeing a client and have another clinician in crisis who needs attention. Also, there are just tons of paperwork, which is mostly done to satisfy various providers and standards that are not really relevant to therapy or the clients' needs.

—Licensed professional counselor, 23 years,
Brownsville, Tennessee

I spend most of my day acting as an advocate for others within our complex and often frustrating legal and regulatory system.

—Social worker, 8 years,
Baltimore, Maryland

About 50 to 60 percent of my time is devoted to clinical therapy sessions, with the remainder divided between management and training duties.

—Licensed clinical social worker, 17 years,
Mesa, Arizona

. . .

What are the best parts of your profession?

Bringing down the level of familial chaos, and directing people back to a degree of normal social interaction.

—Licensed professional counselor, 6 years,
Vicksburg, Mississippi

Reducing the burdens of others and hopefully equipping them with better tools to respond to the next set of social pressures and traumas.

—Licensed clinical social worker, 11 years,
Des Moines, Iowa

For me the most pleasure comes in helping to train and equip the next generation of social workers and therapists.

—Licensed clinical social worker/adjunct college professor, 21 years,
Lexington, Kentucky

. . .

What are the least enjoyable aspects of your profession?

The painful details of stories that you have to listen to, especially from children. It is a very central part of the job, but it is still emotionally draining at a level that you cannot anticipate while in school.

—Licensed clinical social worker, 4 years,
Redmond, Washington

The low pay for the critical work you are playing in others' lives. To remain in the profession for the long haul, you have to carve out a personal reward for yourself that comes from the mere act of seeing suffering lessened in the lives of others.

—Licensed professional counselor, 19 years,
Dothan, Alabama

The cumulative impact on my own emotional stability from being the vehicle through which others release their traumatic experiences. Counselors can be truly effective only if their own lives are stable.

—Licensed clinical social worker, 5 years,
Bristol, Virginia

CHANGES IN THE PROFESSION

What changes do you foresee for your profession?

The major focus of change in our profession has been and will continue to be centered around the impact of managed-care organizations, which will more and more dictate how and to what extent counselors are able to treat their clients. The emphasis is changing from one of applied methodology to one where a solution is achieved.

—Licensed professional counselor, 10 years,
Salem, Oregon

As the roll of uninsured Americans continues to climb, the demand for free counseling programs will increase dramatically. At the same time, the workloads of the existing counselors will only increase as funding is never on par with the demand for our services.

—Licensed clinical social worker, 16 years,
Eau Claire, Wisconsin

The advances in science behind understanding mental illness will hopefully cause the insurance companies to treat mental disorders more in line with how they assess and pay for physical ones.

—Licensed clinical social worker, 11 years, Lynchburg, Virginia

WOULD YOU DO IT ALL OVER AGAIN?

Do you find your daily job fulfilling?

I do. I would not want to be doing anything else with my life. The ability to aid children, adolescents, and families in finding healing now and living more fulfilling and productive lives is the most fulfilling part of my job. Knowing that these individuals will not have to live another day with open wounds but will be able to heal and utilize their scars to make them more compassionate, loving, and fulfilled individuals.

—Licensed clinical social worker, 5 years, Nashville, Tennessee

I find it fluctuates between fulfillment and being emotionally overwhelmed.

—Social worker, 9 years, Midwest City, Oklahoma

I have come to peace with what I do. It is stressful and low paying, but so very necessary in the broad scheme of things.

—Licensed clinical social worker, 14 years, Plano, Texas

. . .

Would you choose the same profession again?

I would. It is what I am meant to do with my life. It is not perfect, but it is where my heart is.

—Social worker, 9 years, Monroe, Louisiana

I am afraid not. Hindsight is always 20/20, but the impact this career has had on my own relationships has been so costly that I wouldn't make the same choice again.

—Licensed clinical social worker, 5 years, Ogden, Utah

Without question. It is my way of giving something back to the world. Without it, I would be incomplete as a person.

—Licensed professional counselor, 14 years, Holyoke, Massachusetts

155

A CAREER IN

Information Technology

SO YOU WANT TO BE A
COMPUTER ENGINEER

The reality of the profession is that political and social forces are just as impor-
tant as the science of our profession, and college does not give you the tools
to anticipate those aspects. In the past five years, information technology has
become a commodity just like raw materials, and the price of IT services is
dictating more than ever before which firms get the business.

Blogs, wikis, social media, portals, HTML, CPUs, chat rooms, pod-
casters, MySpace, YouTube, Flash Gallery — the world of information
technology, or IT, has a language all its own.

Though synonymous with the twenty-first century, computing, at
its most basic, has been around for at least five hundred years. Mechanical calculators were manufactured for sale as early as 1640. Looms that
worked by reading punched holes on small sheets of hardwood were used
in the early 1800s. In the mid-1800s a programmable machine translated
a short written work by Ada Lovelace, who is generally regarded as the
first programmer. In 1854, George Boone, considered the father of
computer science, wrote *An Investigation of the Laws of Thought*. By the

1930s programmable electronic calculating devices were being used in Germany. During World War II, the British built a secret computer, the Colossus Mark I, to break Germany's complex mechanical encoder, the Enigma.

In development through the 1940s, the first computer was patented in the 1950s. Also in the 1950s, Grace Hopper proposed reusable software and gave birth to the concept of compiling data. With the introduction of the transistor and integrated circuits, the age of the computer dawned. In 1969 Alan Keys proposed the first personal computer, and in 1982 *Time* selected the computer as its "Man of the Year." Then, in the 1990s, the internet and the World Wide Web emerged, along with greatly increasing performance levels in the speed, memory capacity, and accuracy of computers. As this happened, the field of computer engineering grew substantially, allowing for the creation of intricate, complex programs and huge networks to solve highly challenging business needs.

From a career perspective today, the world of information technology is divided into two principal categories — software engineers and hardware engineers.

Hardware engineers, or *systems analysts*, specialize in analyzing and planning the entire computer and communications layout for a business or company. This includes recommending appropriate computer hardware, building and modifying product prototypes, and conferring with software engineers to evaluate interfacing between hardware and software as well as maximizing operational and performance requirements. The title "hardware engineer" (as distinct from "systems analyst") also refers to those who supervise the manufacture and installation of all types of computers and computer-related equipment.

Software engineers specialize in customizing existing computer software programs to meet the particular needs of a business or industry; common areas of focus include billing, inventory, shipping, payroll, customer service, and e-commerce. In general, there are two categories of software engineers: *system software engineers* and *applications software engineers*. System software engineers maintain entire computer systems for a company, while application software engineers design, create, or modify general or specialized computer applications. Software engineers sometimes specialize in particular industries, such as insurance, medicine, or the law.

If you are considering becoming a computer engineer, the ability to research, define, and analyze problems is a vital skill; however, there are no particular educational or licensing requirements. Since almost by definition technology is constantly changing, industry certifications have evolved as a way for companies to assess the technical skill sets of both potential and current employees. National examinations are designed in conjunction with major IT companies, such as Microsoft, Novell, Oracle, and Cisco, and they are offered in four main segments of the industry: Windows administration, networking, database management, and wireless. Many employers increase wages based upon the level of certifications achieved, and even pay, in whole or in part, the cost of the classes and courses necessary to complete certifications. However, even if direct compensation is not increased, many IT employees view certifications as a necessary component of bettering your career; securing and keeping an IT job is a process, not an event. Some employers also see a secondary benefit from the certification process, viewing those who are willing to navigate through the certification process as self-starters and go-getters.

In terms of job trends, the outlook is mixed. In 1965, computer scientist and engineer Gordon E. Moore predicted that the memory capacity of semiconductors would double every eighteen months, and his prediction has held true. Technological change has grown exponentially, and the speed of this change has become a defining characteristic of the information age. Job opportunities have also increased in a similarly explosive fashion, but whether that will continue isn't clear. As technology matures and becomes more user-friendly, the general public is learning to use computers and communicate in ways only IT people could just a decade ago. The mysterious world of IT is becoming more approachable by everyone. One by-product of this evolution is what

Thomas Friedman discusses in his bestseller *The World Is Flat* — that the information technology needs of almost any American business can now be performed by people anywhere in the world.

BY THE NUMBERS

EMPLOYMENT LEVELS: According to the U.S. Bureau of Labor Statistics, there are over 1. 1 million individuals employed in the United States in the field of computer systems design and related service industries. This number includes a wide range of occupations, including engineering, systems analysis, programming, technical support, sales, office and administrative support, and management. Of this total, there are 133,000 software engineers, 87,000 systems analysts, and 12,000 hardware engineers.

ACADEMIC REQUIREMENTS: There are no particular requirements for entering the world of information technology. Industry certification examinations designed in association with major IT companies, and administered on a national basis, are available to anyone in the areas of Windows administration, networking, database management, and wireless. However, more and more people entering the IT field have an undergraduate degree in computer science, and many go on to secure a master's in information technology or information systems management.

AVERAGE SALARY LEVELS: According to the U.S. Bureau of Labor Statistics, starting salaries for software engineers are in the mid-**$40,000s**, while those for systems analysts are in the low **$40,000s**. The median income for software engineers is **$79,955**, and for systems analysts it's **$69,555**.

COLLEGE VS. REALITY

How would you compare the reality of your profession to the picture you had of it while in school?

I did not major in computer science in college, but I found that one's ability to think critically is the most important quality. Trial by fire does have its advantages — it weeds out those who can't identify the problem quickly.

—**Technical support manager, 16 years, Irving, Texas**

The reality of the profession is that political and social forces are just as important as the science of our profession, and college does not give you the tools to anticipate those aspects. In the past five years, information technology has become a commodity just like raw materials, and the price of IT services is dictating more than ever before which firms get the business.

—**Software engineer, 10 years, Portland, Oregon**

People ignore the sales side of information technology. Specialized software is a product, whether it is for the accounting field, the legal field, or the medical field. I took business courses and computer science courses, and the combination prepared me well.

—**Vice president of sales, legal/ accounting software firm, 22 years, Overland Park, Kansas**

· · ·

How would you rate your collegiate and graduate courses in preparing you for your profession on a scale of 1 to 10, with 10 being the best?

10. My degree has taught me how to logically look at any situation and find a viable way to automate the process. I was taught how to program, so it's very easy for me to learn the most up-to-date programming language.

—**Software engineer, 20 years, Orlando, Florida**

7, but in a broad context. My education prepared me for systems improvement regardless of the industry or the information technology application.

—**Systems analyst, 24 years, Portland, Oregon**

6. My courses gave me a good foundation, but it is the art of problem solving and critical thinking that makes me most effective in my profession.

—**Computer engineer/systems analyst, 9 years, Springfield, Missouri**

THE BIGGEST SURPRISE

What most surprised you about your chosen profession?

How quickly things have changed since 2000. What appeared to be a wide-open field full of opportunities has now become a narrowing field, at least in the United States, with stagnant pay rates.

—Software engineer, 8 years,
Albany, New York

How American government policies created an environment that promoted the outsourcing of American IT jobs.

—Software engineer, 12 years,
Phoenix, Arizona

The incredible pace with which technology has advanced.

—Systems analyst/IT consultant, 33 years,
Medford, Massachusetts

HOURS AND ADVANCEMENT

How many hours do you work each week at your career?

Sixty. That's what it takes when running your own business.

—President of website design and
interactive media firm, 16 years,
Lexington, Kentucky

Forty-five.

—Software engineer, 11 years,
Montclair, New Jersey

Fifty.

—Systems analyst, 16 years, Tucson, Arizona

. . .

Have you found advancement within your career easy or difficult?

Tough. It is a very competitive business.

—Software design consultant, 26 years,
Milwaukee, Wisconsin

Very difficult. As a woman I have found that the glass ceiling is impenetrable.

—Technical support manager, 15 years,
Columbus, Ohio

It was much easier five years ago to find advancement.

—Software engineer, 21 years,
Newport News, Virginia

THE BEST AND THE WORST

What do you spend most of your day doing? Describe a typical day.

Communication with clients, establishing requirements, clarifying issues, emailing and talking with clients and staff (consulting) in providing technical and nontechnical solutions.

—Systems analyst, 18 years,
Altamonte Springs, Florida

My days are usually made of one or more of three central tasks: technical analysis, development, or testing.

—Software engineer, 14 years,
Norman, Oklahoma

Respond to emails and phone calls that never end, and assign individuals to respond to service calls. If you are good at technical support, there is a lot of business out there. But beware, the stress levels are high, customers are many times frantic, and they expect you to be available 24/7.

—Technical support manager, 12 years,
New Britain, Connecticut

. . .

What are the best parts of your profession?

The intellectual challenge.

—Software engineer, 9 years,
Charleston, South Carolina

Providing a positive impact for my clients by fashioning a solution that best suits their particular needs.

—Owner, interactive media firm, 12 years,
Philadelphia, Pennsylvania

The constant change in technology, and the enjoyment of always learning and then applying that knowledge to real-world solutions.

—Hardware engineer, 17 years,
Austin, Texas

. . .

What are the least enjoyable aspects of your profession?

From a broad perspective, the continued outsourcing of technology jobs overseas and fewer and fewer opportunities for new people to get into the IT industry.

—Software engineer, 12 years,
Rockford, Illinois

Being controlled by the needs of our customers. By solving our customers' technical problems at a high level, I have boxed myself in and been unable to move up in the company because management is afraid that they cannot replace me. It is the classic catch-22.

—Customer support manager, 14 years,
Marietta, Georgia

Collecting unpaid accounts.

—Owner, website design firm/interactive
media consultant, 11 years,
Charlotte, North Carolina

CHANGES IN THE PROFESSION

What changes do you foresee for your profession?

The biggest change in our profession will continue to be one word — India. We have lost our bargaining power; nobody respects nerds anymore. Granted, it was grudging respect: we could do absolute magic. But we were always suspect because the suits couldn't understand us, but they needed us, so they had to show at least a façade of respect. . . . Now, they don't have to.

—IT customer support manager, 18 years, Boulder, Colorado

Customers paying monthly fees instead of large investments in hardware and software.

—CEO, medical software firm, 41 years, Chattanooga, Tennessee

More specialization in various aspects of the industry. Easier-to-use-and-maintain hardware and software that require fewer workers.

—IT director, interactive media firm, 9 years, Orlando, Florida

WOULD YOU DO IT ALL OVER AGAIN?

Do you find your daily job fulfilling?

Yes; there is always a new challenge to complete.

—Software engineer, 18 years, Memphis, Tennessee

Day to day, I am not all that fulfilled. Yet when I step back and look at my work after completing a challenging assignment, I realize that this field is where I belong.

—Operations and systems consultant, 19 years, Dayton, Ohio

Yes. Like Ben Kingsley's character said to Robert Redford's character in the movie *Sneakers*, the power comes from controlling the information. I want to be on the forefront of that power, not on the outside looking in.

—Computer engineer/consultant, 21 years, Nashville, Tennessee

. . .

Would you choose the same profession again?

If I did, I would focus on the operations side, and not the technical side.

—IT technical support manager, 14 years, Bakersfield, California

No. I would go into a field that could not be outsourced to people in other countries. There is one, right?

—Software engineer, 8 years, Baton Rouge, Louisiana

Yes. I did not complete my college education, but the field of information technology provided me the opportunity to rise through the ranks — from technical support to operations management to chief information officer of a major company — based on my own abilities to complete industry certifications at higher and higher levels and to create solutions for IT needs as our company grew nationally and internationally.

—Chief information officer, 16 years, Chicago, Illinois

CAREERS IN

Sales and Marketing

SO YOU WANT TO BE A MARKETING MANAGER

I never imagined I would be sitting in front of a computer crunching numbers nearly as much as I do. I thought data analysis would consume approximately a quarter of my time, as opposed to three-quarters-plus of my time. I also thought I would design and implement more advertising and marketing plans, as opposed to coordinating with an advertising agency to do that.

Some estimate that almost 25 percent of all workers worldwide are involved in some phase of marketing, using the term in the broadest sense. This includes all the retailers, salespersons, manufacturer's representatives, wholesalers, advertisers, promoters, marketing managers, and so on.

This chapter focuses on marketing managers. These are the people who determine the demand for products and services offered by a company, and who identify customers for these products and services. Many people confuse the professions of advertising and marketing, and indeed, depending on the size of a business, the line between these activities can easily become blurred. In general, advertising is an attempt to persuade an audience to purchase a particular good or utilize a particular service. Advertising in America dates back to colonial times, when advertisements for products appeared in Benjamin Franklin's *Pennsylvania Gazette*. Marketing, on the other hand, focuses more on the customer than on the product; it consists of identifying customers and their needs and strategizing ways the business can satisfy them and hopefully build a sustained relationship for the benefit of all. Another distinction is that, in larger and more established businesses, marketing managers are usually company employees, while advertising duties are usually performed by outside agencies.

The role of marketing manager differs depending on which aspect of marketing is pursued. One such role is that of brand management. In most large companies, each brand name is managed as a unique business, with brand managers responsible for planning, developing, and directing the market mix associated with the name. The more expertly the brand name is managed, the more opportunities exist to offer new product lines.

Take Nike, for example. Originally known as Blue Ribbon Sports in the mid-1960s, the company was based upon an idea for a lighter and yet more durable running shoe. Then, in the early 1970s, founder Phil Knight changed the name to Nike, for the winged goddess of victory in Greek mythology. While teaching at Portland State University, he asked a student doing some freelance work to come up with a graphic design, or logo, that could be placed on the side of the shoe. She handed him the "swoosh," which was meant to embody the spirit of the winged goddess. With the new name and logo, sales reached $1 million in the early 1970s, and by 1996, when Nike was named the "Marketer of the Year," sales had reached a staggering $6.74 billion, and the company sold a wide array of products, each bearing the now-ubiquitous swoosh. The success of Nike is a marketing case study of brilliantly tapping into the mind and desires of the consumer, which include a deep-rooted yearning for cultural inclusiveness and, in this case, a desire to strive for, or at least emulate, athletic accomplishment.

Marketing managers can also be involved in retail marketing. This type of marketing career offers opportunities in merchandising, central management, and product purchasing. Others become market researchers, utilizing surveys, new product tests, statistical packages, and focus groups to help determine what makes consumers select certain products.

The role of a marketing manager is multifaceted. On any given day it can involve consulting with product development personnel on the specifications for the newest line of products; working with advertisers to develop a promotional plan; communicating with vendors and distributors to assure manufacturing quotas and product distribution networks; data analysis of sales forecasts and projections (crunching the numbers); consulting with retail buyers to gain information as to what products or services are expected by the ever-evolving marketplace; and coordinating and participating in trade shows and other promotional events.

What knowledge and attributes contribute to a successful marketer? There are no degree or licensing requirements to become a marketing manager, but a good grasp of marketing, advertising, and business are essential, whether acquired in school or on the job. Marketers need to know the principles of promoting and selling, they need to be able to spot consumer trends, and they need to understand financial forecasting. Good written and oral communication skills are a must, as is the ability to multitask and to work to deadlines and budgets.

A career in marketing also offers an opportunity to participate, on a broader scale, in shaping the society in which we live. On one level, successful marketing, which builds demand for a certain product, creates and grows businesses, which creates more jobs and improves local economies. On another level, marketers can become taste-makers and actually change societal behavior. Marketing doesn't always mean selling products. For instance, the antismoking campaign that has swept America in the past decade or so is partly the result of smart, and successful, marketing.

BY THE NUMBERS

EMPLOYMENT LEVELS: According to the U.S. Bureau of Labor Statistics, there are currently 167,000 marketing managers in the United States.

ACADEMIC REQUIREMENTS: There are no specific academic requirements to become a marketing manager. However, most companies prefer marketers to have concentrated their academic studies in marketing, advertising, and business.

AVERAGE SALARY LEVELS: According to the National Association of Colleges and Employers, the average starting salary for marketing majors is **$33,783**. The profession does allow for substantial income growth. The U.S. Bureau of Labor Statistics estimates that the median annual earnings for marketing managers are **$87,640**.

COLLEGE VS. REALITY

How would you compare the reality of your profession to the picture you had of it while in school?

I had always been interested in new products and was constantly looking in magazines to see how products were being marketed. College gave me the basics that you can apply to almost any product, but each industry, and for that matter each company, has its own unique methods and issues.

—Brand marketing assistant vice president,
Fortune 500 company, 6 years,
Alpharetta, Georgia

College is idealist in its presentation. I envisioned marketing to be much more of a creative profession, where in reality the constant need to "make the numbers" morphs the profession into more of your typical corporate cubicle office job, and a large part of the creative side, which is what attracted me to marketing in school, is outsourced to creative ad agencies.

—Retail marketing manager,
national clothing chain, 11 years,
Dallas, Texas

I think school should teach more classes about real life and finance.

—Wholesale HVAC sales and marketing,
12 years, Bartlett, Tennessee

. . .

How would you rate your collegiate and graduate courses in preparing you for your profession on a scale of 1 to 10, with 10 being the best?

8. Various business courses laid the foundation and exposed me to skills I would later need. Accounting, statistics, and economics still play a daily part in my business life. The history and liberal arts courses I took also play a part in my professional life, in that my word skills and wide breadth of life exposures afford me openings in conversation with a wide and varied base of clients, regardless of their status in life or business.

—Global sales and marketing manager,
40 years, Carmel, Indiana

College gave me the fundamentals, but only in a real-world setting will you be able to fit all the pieces together.

—Assistant marketing manager, 3 years,
Brookfield, Wisconsin

A good general overview, but not enough emphasis on how many different issues you deal with as a marketer, from production issues all the way to special promotions.

—Marketing assistant vice president,
5 years, Warwick, Rhode Island

THE BIGGEST SURPRISE

What most surprised you about your chosen profession?

I never imagined I would be sitting in front of a computer crunching numbers nearly as much as I do. I thought data analysis would consume approximately a quarter of my time, as opposed to three-quarters-plus of my time. I also thought I would design and implement more advertising and marketing plans, as opposed to coordinating with an advertising agency to do that.

—Assistant marketing manager,
Fortune 500 company, 1 year,
Winston-Salem, North Carolina

The amount of stress that comes with the job. It is something you can't appreciate until you experience it first-hand.

**—Marketing vice president, 12 years,
Roanoke, Virginia**

The spread of income available from the low-end entrance to the supreme top job.

**—Sales, marketing, and distribution
executive, 31 years, El Dorado, Arkansas**

HOURS AND ADVANCEMENT

How many hours do you work each week at your career?

Sixty to sixty-five, and for a very average salary.

**—Marketing department, small marketing
firm, 4 years, Columbia, South Carolina**

Forty-five to fifty if in the office, but during weeks when I attend trade shows or other industry functions, it becomes fifty-five to sixty.

**—Assistant marketing manager,
home improvement product, 5 years,
Dubuque, Iowa**

Forty-five to fifty-five.

**—Marketing manager, 14 years,
Canton, Massachusetts**

. . .

Have you found advancement within your career easy or difficult?

I felt that advancement would prove a viable option based on the feedback I had received from my boss. Then we experienced a downsizing. I still have my job, but my boss and lots of other middle managers got fired.

**—Assistant marketing manager,
Fortune 500 company, 3 years,
Norcross, Georgia**

If you work for a large company, like I do, you are compensated well, but you are given huge responsibilities. If you handle them well, you can advance. The problem is that cost-containment themes are constantly shoved in front of you. So in the back of your mind, there is always this career instability that is hovering in the air. Everyone, and I mean everyone, is replaceable.

—Brand marketing, 12 years, Irving, Texas

There are no free rides out there. Once you have a seat at the table, you have to constantly perform. There is always someone under you eyeing your position. If you want the freedom to control your own destiny, start your own firm — if you have the guts.

**—Marketing vice president, 14 years,
Indianapolis, Indiana**

THE BEST AND THE WORST

What do you spend most of your day doing? Describe a typical day.

Analyzing numbers, putting out fires — like production issues or shipping problems — assisting in developing catalogues for our products, and meetings and more meetings.

—**Marketing vice president, 17 years,**
Winter Park, Florida

Talking to customers to best meet their needs, conceptualizing new promotional ideas to better move product, and meeting with my boss and others in the company to see if we are meeting projections, and if not, why not.

—**Assistant marketing manager, 2 years,**
Springfield, Massachusetts

On the phone with and emailing various suppliers, attending trade shows, and trying to always stay ahead of the curve with the latest fashions and products.

—**Retail marketing, regional clothier,**
15 years, Lexington, Kentucky

. . .

What are the best parts of your profession?

If you are lucky enough to go to work for a marketing-driven company as compared to a sales-driven company, you realize that you have the opportunity to have a direct impact on the financial well-being of the company, if not day to day, at least quarter to quarter.

—**Marketing vice president, 12 years,**
Redding, California

The opportunity to be on the cutting edge of the latest designs and product ideas, and to offer up ideas to maximize their delivery to the marketplace.

—**Marketing vice president,**
knitwear manufacturer, 14 years, New York

When I am able to use my creativity to help improve the overall delivery of a product in one or more phases, from production to promotion.

—**Assistant marketing manager, outerwear**
manufacturer, 4 years, Portland, Oregon

. . .

What are the least enjoyable aspects of your profession?

The pressure to succeed — people's jobs depend on my success or failure.

—**Sales/marketing senior vice president,**
furniture manufacturing, 38 years,
Atlanta, Georgia

Meetings, meetings, meetings. My life is one series of meetings, and yet somehow I am expected to get all my work done as well.

—**Assistant marketing manager,**
Fortune 1000 company, 10 years,
Louisville, Kentucky

The lack of individual identity that this job affords. Only the executives end up making the long-term connections with clients.

—**Assistant marketing manager, 4 years,**
Silver Spring, Maryland

CHANGES IN THE PROFESSION

What changes do you foresee for your profession?

Customers have and will continue to become more demanding.

—Regional sales/marketing manager,
national manufacturer, 7 years,
Nashville, Tennessee

More and more outsourcing of what was once in-house work on a contract basis.

—Assistant marketing manager, 4 years,
Fort Worth, Texas

The need to think globally in your marketing efforts.

—Wholesale marketing manager, 16 years,
Farmington, Michigan

WOULD YOU DO IT ALL OVER AGAIN?

Do you find your daily job fulfilling?

It is rewarding to help a customer be more successful, but I don't find individual fulfillment in my job. The creative aspects that attracted me are too often drowned by the constant financial demands to meet the numbers.

—Marketing assistant, 2 years,
Lansing, Michigan

I am one of many on the marketing side of my large corporate company. Initially I was eager to conquer the world with all my creative juices flowing, but after four years on the job, I realize that if I were to drop off the face of the earth tomorrow, they would simply find someone else to perform my duties. There is no real camaraderie. We are all just spokes in a very large set of corporate wheels.

—Assistant marketing manager, 4 years,
Chicago, Illinois

I like the people I work with, and a positive side of my job is the team efforts that I lead. I realize that my marketing skills have a direct impact on the bottom line.

—Marketing/product development,
regional company, 15 years,
Spartanburg, South Carolina

. . .

Would you choose the same profession again?

Yes, I would stay in marketing, but I would search for a smaller firm where I could have a greater impact and a greater opportunity to use my creative talents.

—Market research manager, 10 years,
Phoenix, Arizona

No. I would go into business for myself, where I had much more control over the product mix and the promotion of the products. You can be stimulated for only so long marketing a product that sits on a counter.

**—Marketing manager, 9 years,
Pittsburgh, Pennsylvania**

"Marketing" is a very broad term. I would try to find a company that was part advertising and part marketing, rather than work for a large corporation selling the same product that many others are selling.

**—Brand marketing department,
national company, 7 years, Cleveland, Ohio**

SO YOU WANT TO BE A PUBLIC RELATIONS SPECIALIST

Public relations is all about the world of communication. And that is how I spend most of my day — communicating with someone, by email, on the phone, or in person. Whether it is participating with my coworkers in creating an effective campaign for a client or implementing that campaign, my day is all about communicating. If you want your day to be one that allows for a lot of quiet reflective creativity, PR is not for you. This is a world that epitomizes the art of blending creativity with fast-paced decisions.

When a movie star makes a racial slur, a politician spouts nonsensical factoids, a professional athlete gets caught driving drunk, a public company's earnings are below Wall Street's expectations, or a manufacturer's product threatens the public's health, who gets the call? That's right. A public relations specialist jumps into action to present the most favorable image and interpretation possible — placing a positive spin on any negative situation. In our media-saturated world, when every embarrassing slip seems to find its way onto the internet, a good PR firm seems as necessary as a cell phone.

Public relations firms aren't only called upon to slap a smiley face on bad news. They actually work on a wide variety of corporate, institutional, and business issues, promoting events, good deeds, and important plans. For example, if a university plans to expand its facilities in a way that will impact the community or nearby private residences, the university will ask a public relations firm to help strategize the best ways to present their plan at neighborhood meetings, to the city fathers, and to the school's alumni. If a national nonprofit organization seeks to roll out a new public health initiative, a public relations firm can help it present the program through national media as well as develop ways to get large employers to participate. If a corporation elects to close a major plant, the company will consult with a public relations firm on how to handle the closing and the best way to deflect any negative reaction.

Full-service public relations firms are now often referred to as communications companies, and they break their services down into a number of categories, like *strategic planning*, *community relations*, *crisis management*, *media relations*, *promotions*, *event planning*, and *media training*.

In general, the needs of the client determine what a public relations specialist does, and PR people can specialize in many diverse ways. Some specialize in the public opinion aspects of a certain industry, others in a type of PR, like media relations or event planning. Others become lobbyists, who work to persuade legislators rather than the public. While the field is dominated by private firms, many large companies, especially publicly held ones, also have their own internal public relations officers.

The day-to-day life of a public relations specialist can include any of the following activities: writing news releases, speeches, and copy for radio, television, or the internet; editing employee publications, newsletters, and other management communications; contacting the press, radio, television, and internet outlets to arrange for media coverage of an event; handling corporate communications at special events, press parties, and conventions; determining appropriate public platforms for company officials; recommending the public relations steps in presenting and carrying out a company program; consulting with advertisers in the presentation and promotion of a company's name and reputation; and developing specific brochures, booklets, and photographic presentations for a corporate goal, program, or position.

As with marketing, there is no specific academic degree required to become a public relations specialist. The heart of public relations is effective communication, so courses or work experience that improve your communication skills are key to a successful career. English, journalism, and public speaking are all relevant areas of study, plus there are now over two hundred colleges and universities with programs or special courses in public relations.

In addition to good communication skills, it helps to know something about the industry or company you are representing. In fact, it is not unusual for someone who has worked in one field, such as banking or science, to leave his or her profession and enter the world of public relations as a spokesperson for that particular industry or a large employer within that industry. The better a public relations specialist understands the business operations of clients, the more effective he or she will be.

BY THE NUMBERS

EMPLOYMENT LEVELS: According to the U.S. Bureau of Labor Statistics, there are 243,000 salaried employees in the field of public relations. They are concentrated in advertising and related services, health care, educational services, communications firms, financial institutions, and government offices.

ACADEMIC REQUIREMENTS: There are no specific academic requirements for becoming a public relations specialist. However, the competition is keen, and those with college degrees majoring in public relations, journalism, advertising, or communication are most sought after. Also, internships and co-op programs are highly encouraged. One organization that works with universities to assist with internship positions is the Public Relations Student Society of America.

AVERAGE SALARY LEVELS: According to the U.S. Bureau of Labor Statistics, the median annual salary for a public relations specialist is **$43,830**; the average salary range is **$25,750** to **$80,120**.

COLLEGE VS. REALITY

How would you compare the reality of your profession to the picture you had of it while in school?

In college, there is this undefined glamour or mystique that surrounds the entire advertising and public relations field. The glamour quickly wears off with the stress of meeting deadlines and the bouncing from one project to another, along with the average pay.

—Communications specialist, 4 years,
Arlington, Texas

In school you are more focused on the creative side. In the real world, when the economy is good, you are having to constantly perform quickly and decisively. When the economy is bad, there are layoffs in broad strokes.

—Account executive, marketing and PR firm,
13 years, Arlington, Virginia

I find the day-to-day job to be much more stimulating than I envisioned while in school. Many times you are a key member of a team that is diffusing a negative turn of events that has the potential to dramatically affect the entire future of a business. At times, it can be sort of be like working in the ER room of a business world.

—Public relations specialist, 3 years,
Sandy Springs, Georgia

. . .

How would you rate your collegiate and graduate courses in preparing you for your profession on a scale of 1 to 10, with 10 being the best?

College can prepare you for a public relations career in a broad sense, and courses in public relations, journalism, marketing, and advertising are all helpful, but it is the ability to persuade people with your ideas that is the heart of public relations. That is a talent college can possibly improve but not really teach.

—Communications specialist, 4 years,
Charleston, South Carolina

6. It gave me a good background. What it lacked was the art of politics. PR should really be called the people relations business because it is for other people that you are getting the message out. It is your version, but it is your client's message. You have to be creative and confident in your presentation but let the people you are working for still feel they are in control. They are the ones paying the bill.

—Media specialist, 7 years,
San Jose, California

This is not brain surgery. Some of the best PR people in the business were the worst students in school. They partied and had lots of friends. Having good social skills is essential to being effective in this business. In public relations you are telling a story — someone else's story. The people who hire you have to like you and believe that you can make the public like what you are saying on their behalf.

—Account executive, 11 years,
Wilmington Delaware

THE BIGGEST SURPRISE

What most surprised you about your chosen profession?

I felt that my creative ideas would be much more individually recognized by the actual clients. Instead, I am just one of the worker bees, and the head of our firm gets the glory. There is much more politics to all of this than I anticipated.

—Account executive, communications firm,
5 years, Chicago, Illinois

How many women are in the public relations business.

—Account coordinator, 2 years,
Germantown, Tennessee

The fast-paced environment. It is like cooking a seven-course meal. You have to be sure nothing burns, but you have to give each project the concentrated effort it needs.

—Public relations specialist, 3 years,
Pittsburgh, Pennsylvania

HOURS AND ADVANCEMENT

How many hours do you work each week at your career?

It varies depending on the needs of your clients. If an event has to be coordinated in a short time frame, a forty-five-hour week can quickly stretch into a sixty-hour week or more.

—Account executive, public relations firm,
11 years, Tacoma, Washington

It depends on what issues I have to deal with, but on average it is forty-five to fifty.

—Communications specialist, 9 years,
San Antonio, Texas

It depends to a large degree on where you work within a large firm. If you are involved in the marketing communications plans department or the media training department, your workweek has some stability to it. If you work in crisis communications or event planning, you are more often called upon to work odd hours.

—Public relations specialist, 4 years,
Scottsdale, Arizona

. . .

Have you found advancement within your career easy or difficult?

Advancement within the public relations department of a large corporation is difficult because there are traditionally very few individuals within that department, and people become entrenched.

—Communications director, 17 years,
Roswell, Georgia

As in most professions, advancement is predicated upon performance. Those that advance the most quickly are either the most creative souls or those that garner the most new business. But be ready; the world of public relations firms is highly competitive.

—Public relations specialist, 9 years,
Denver, Colorado

There is only so far you can climb up the public relations ladder in a small firm, unless you are invited to have an ownership position in your company.

—Media specialist, 15 years,
Richmond, Virginia

THE BEST AND THE WORST

What do you spend most of your day doing? Describe a typical day.

Public relations is all about the world of communication. And that is how I spend most of my day — communicating with someone, by email, on the phone, or in person. Whether it is participating with my coworkers in creating an effective campaign for a client or implementing that campaign, my day is all about communicating. If you want your day to be one that allows for a lot of quiet reflective creativity, PR is not for you. This is a world that epitomizes the art of blending creativity with fast-paced decisions.

—Communications specialist, 13 years,
Winter Park, Florida

Meeting with my coworkers to be sure the campaigns for my accounts are on track; working my existing relationships and contacts and making the phone calls necessary to position my accounts with the right mix of outdoor, direct mail, media buys, and online exposure to accomplish their goals.

—Account executive, 7 years,
Boston, Massachusetts

Meeting with new clients to assess their communications, marketing, and public relations needs, working with my staff to oversee and review design and creative campaigns to best suit our clients' goals, monitoring the progress of all our major accounts, and keeping the name of our firm out front in the community by involving myself with as many boards and committees as my calendar permits.

—Executive vice president, marketing and
PR firm, 17 years, Kansas City, Kansas

. . .

What are the best parts of your profession?

Because I work for a nonprofit, getting the message out takes on a whole new level of importance. When I get to work with a volunteer or I hear that someone has benefited from hearing the message, it makes the struggle worthwhile.

—Communications director, 5 years,
Nashville, Tennessee

I have been able to use my writing skills more than I anticipated. My talents for writing effectively and within a deadline were recognized by my superiors, and I have been able to carve out an enjoyable niche where I specialize in creating newsletters for our customers and also working on larger writing projects such as internal employee communication manuals.

—Communications specialist, 6 years,
Beaverton, Oregon

I am able to have a recognizable impact on the health of a company's communications. Some organizations become so large that they lose touch with their own employees. When major events occur for a large organization, most think outwardly as to the best way to present the event or its impact to their customers and to the community. Now with the help of internal campaigns, staged employee gatherings, and well-crafted newsletters, our firm has been able to improve the communications between companies and the people that keep them running and growing.

—Account executive, public relations firm,
15 years, Washington, D.C.

. . .

What are the least enjoyable aspects of your profession?

The pressure and stress!!! Many times you will have only a matter of weeks to create an effective campaign that diffuses a major event or corporate development, the negative impact from which can severely scar the business reputation of an established business.

—Public relations specialist, 6 years,
Sugar Land, Texas

Not feeling that my talents are being fully utilized. I work for a large corporation, and yet the communications department is a very small one. Marketing always wants to be out front on things, and we seemed to be called in only when things have gone poorly. If we were brought in more on the front end, the executive committee would be able to better see our value to the company.

—Communications specialist, 4 years,
Hartford, Connecticut

The politics of the job. I spend so much of my day dealing with people's egos, including the clients' and the media connections', that it dilutes the more enjoyable parts of this profession.

—Media specialist, 10 years, New York City

CHANGES IN THE PROFESSION

What changes do you foresee for your profession?

The fast-paced changes in technology will present more new ways to get the word out. Being creative so as to maximize the newest features in terms of communicating your message will be one key to being most effective for your clients.

—Account executive, communications firm,
7 years, St. Louis, Missouri

A broadening of the role of the communications specialist to include many of the functions of what were once segmented as marketing and advertising. Clients want to use as few consultants as possible, and the more services a firm can offer — such as employee communications, newsletters, the management of advertising and media buys, direct mail, and logo and website development — the better chance a firm has to grow.

—Senior vice president, marketing and PR,
17 years, Los Angeles, California

A consolidation of smaller PR firms into the ranks of larger communications firms. Just a few years ago the majority of PR firms had less than seven employees. Just as banks now offer their customers insurance products and brokerage services, midsize corporate clients will look more and more for a communications firm that can handle its overall marketing and public relations affairs.

—Senior account executive, communications
firm, 12 years, Louisville, Kentucky

WOULD YOU DO IT ALL OVER AGAIN?

Do you find your daily job fulfilling?

Some people respond well to pressure situations. I am one of them. It gets my blood flowing. I like the challenge of having to be creative within a short window of opportunity. Being in public relations allows me to feel connected to the pulse of my community, which helps me to better position the message of our clients.

—Media specialist, 9 years,
Philadelphia, Pennsylvania

On the creative side I did. On the financial side, not as much. More than in some industries, employee rosters grow and shrink dramatically, based on the overall economy. If you work for a private firm and have no desire to be part of the management, you find yourself quite dispensable. There are always lots of younger creative types banging on the door that want to set the world on fire.

—Former public relations specialist,
11 years, Miami, Florida

I don't know of another job that suits my personality and talents better. It keeps me engaged, and I meet and get to work with a lot of interesting people. My job also allows me to stay connected and involved in my community, which adds another dimension to my life.

—Account executive, 8 years,
Indianapolis, Indiana

. . .

Would you choose the same profession again?

No. I would go into media production. After training scores of corporate execs how to not make a complete ass out of themselves when the shit hits the company fan and the media come banging on the door, there is only so much one can derive from this job. There will always be a need for PR people because the boardroom types are usually not media savvy. But being a handler or fixer or mouthpiece for someone else gets old. If I am going to pull someone's ass out of the fire, I would prefer it be my own for a change.

—Media specialist, 15 years, New York City

Yes. The need for a good corporate image has never been more important, thanks to Ken Lay, Bernie Ebbers, Dennis Kozlowski, and John Rigas. What were once public relations firms are now communications firms. The role of the communications specialist is broadening, and the general outlook for the profession is bright.

—Vice president, communications firm,
12 years, Orlando, Florida

Absolutely. I don't know any other profession that would pay me the income I am making with the limited expertise which I possess. I cannot design a bridge, I cannot perform surgery, and I do not know my way around a courtroom. I have taken the same talents that got me elected college sorority president and parlayed them into a successful and lucrative career. I am good with people, can talk with anyone about any matter, put on one hell of an event, think best under pressure, know how to surround myself with excellent people, and build and maintain lasting relationships.

—**Executive vice president,
communications firm, 18 years,
Atlanta, Georgia**

SO YOU WANT TO BE A REALTOR

People think you should be available 24/7. Thanks to cell phones and access to the internet, you are expected to always be available, so it is almost impossible to unplug. You are taught that the call or email you miss may be the next big deal.

When housing prices rise, nearly everyone wants to be in real estate. From 1995 to 2005, historically low interest rates fueled a long-term real estate boom in the United States, with only the horrific events of September 11, 2001, causing a brief downturn for several months. The National Association of Realtors (NAR), which formed in 1908, notes that nearly 25 percent of its current membership received their real estate license between 2005 and 2007. These members include real estate brokers, real estate agents, property managers, appraisers, and others.

Yet, as any seasoned realtor will tell you, the real estate industry is highly cyclical. When mortgage rates rise and the economy stagnates, or when increases in home prices outstrip increases in wages, home buyers stop buying. All those things are in the process of happening in 2008. New housing starts are declining, residential foreclosures are up, the economy is close to a recession, and the nation's largest builder recently laid off thousands of workers.

It's traditionally been said that the three most important things when selling property are location, location, and location. But this could be just as easily changed to timing, timing, and timing. Keep this in mind as you consider whether, and when, to pursue a future in real estate.

Unlike with many professions, being a realtor does not require that you participate full-time. Many housewives and individuals who have retired from other jobs engage in the listing and sale of real estate on a part-time basis. With commission rates across the country averaging 6 percent of the sales price, and with the medium home price in the United States (as of 2006) at $246,500 (compared to $140,000 just a decade earlier and $21,400 in 1966), individuals can make a reasonable living with only a few closings a year. But there is another saying in the world of real estate: 10 percent of realtors make 90 percent of the income. Realtors who fall within that 10 percent typically work seven days a week, 365 days a year, and can make as much as $250,000 to $1 million a year selling all types of properties.

A career in real estate can be very lucrative, but it can take several years to become sufficiently established to achieve this. Virtually all realtors are paid on commission at the time of the consummation of a sale, so until you are established, paychecks can be few and far apart.

The real estate industry is primarily divided into two principal categories — *brokers* and *agents* (or salespersons). Each requires the completion of certain professional courses, with the level of study for brokers being considerably more rigorous. Still, compared to those for most professions, the academic requirements are quite minimal. To be a broker or an agent, you also must be licensed by your home state and participate in certain annual continuing education courses.

Brokers traditionally own and operate real estate companies, and the agents go out and list and sell properties. When a property is sold, the real estate commission is divided between the broker and the agent at a predetermined percentage. These percentages vary from city to city, and sometimes from office to office. Generally, the greater the number of closings that an agent participates in during any given year, the less the amount the broker will receive from each sale. In return for receiving a percentage of each sale, the broker provides the agent with office space and support staff.

A real estate transaction is usually brought together by two different agents. As an example, in the typical residential home sale, one agent represents the sellers of the home, and one agent represents the buyers. Occasionally, only one agent will represent both parties. A prospective buyer who calls the realtor's name on the For Sale sign is calling the seller's agent, and this agent may represent the buyer as well if the buyer doesn't have an agent already, and after proper disclosures as to potential conflicts of interest. Alternatively, prospective buyers might first contact an agent in a particular city, who then finds them properties to see and represents them in a sale.

Most real estate sales also involve two different contracts. The first is the listing contract, or listing agreement. This is the agreement between the party selling the property and the real estate company as the selling broker and establishes the selling price and the level of commission. The second contract is the sales and purchase agreement. This is the contract between the sellers and the buyers, and it states the agreed-on purchase price and all other terms of the sale. The more listings you have as a realtor, the more opportunities you have to generate income.

As with many professions, realtors specialize. Most are in residential sales, but some specialize in commercial properties or industrial properties, and others work only as leasing agents. A realtor can also elect to become a property manager, such as for an office building, a condominium complex, or a retirement community.

BY THE NUMBERS

EMPLOYMENT LEVELS: The National Association of Realtors has over 1.3 million member Realtors, who participate in 1,600 local and 54 state and territorial associations.

ACADEMIC REQUIREMENTS: There are no formal academic degrees necessary to become a realtor. Each state licenses realtors to work in that state; this involves passing a state examination and attending certain required professional courses.

AVERAGE SALARY LEVELS: A realtor's income is commission driven, with commissions being paid upon the closing of the sale. According to the National Association of Realtors, the median annual income level for agents with less than two years' experience is **$15,300**; those with sixteen or more years, experience average **$76,200**. Overall, the average annual income for all realtors in the United States is **$47,700**.

COLLEGE VS. REALITY

How would you compare the reality of your profession to the picture you had of it while in school?

Unlike most careers from which you have the potential to make six-figure incomes, real estate does not require a college degree, so whatever impressions one has of the industry before entering it usually come from others they know working in real estate or from their own experiences in buying or selling a home.

—**Real estate broker, 18 years, Atlanta, Georgia**

I took various business courses in college, some of which touched on the profession of real estate, but they had almost no practical application. Being a successful realtor is more about hard work and being good with people. They don't teach that in school.

—**Commercial realtor, 12 years, Cincinnati, Ohio**

There is no one picture of being a realtor that fits the real world, because being a realtor and being a successful realtor are two different things. A thorough and working knowledge of the basics is helpful, but this is not brain surgery. Once they learn the basics, I can make anyone successful in real estate if they are motivated and willing to work sixty hours a week for the next three years.

—Real estate broker, 20 years,
Chicago, Illinois

. . .

How would you rate your collegiate and graduate (or professional) courses in preparing you for your profession on a scale of 1 to 10, with 10 being the best?

4. The professional courses covered the major areas of real estate, including contracts, calculations, and real estate laws. However, what would be just as, if not more, helpful would be courses on marketing and negotiations.

—Realtor, 12 years, Longview, Texas

The real estate courses that I took for my real estate license gave me the proper language, terms, and laws that apply, but until you are out there working with real people on all sides of the transaction, you are not really learning the reality of the world of real estate.

—Real estate agent, 2 years,
Raleigh, North Carolina

Licensing school taught me a bunch of useless information, and nothing about how to make a home seller/buyer have a better experience.

—Realtor, 18 years, Tulsa, Oklahoma

THE BIGGEST SURPRISE

What most surprised you about your chosen profession?

The number of people who have a real estate license but are not really serious about producing.

—Real estate broker, 21 years,
Cordova, Tennessee

How much harder it is to get established than I thought it would be. Securing a broad client base from which referrals can flow takes years, not months.

—Realtor, 2 years, Peoria, Illinois

The fact that people think you should be available 24/7. Thanks to cell phones and access to the internet, you are expected to always be available, so it is almost impossible to unplug. You are taught that the call or email you miss may be the next big deal.

—Realtor, 4 years,
Springfield, Massachusetts

HOURS AND ADVANCEMENT

How many hours do you work each week at your career?

Fifty to sixty. You can push along the details of each contract only if you are available to solve the problems as they arise, and problems do not occur only nine-to-five, Monday to Friday.

—Realtor, 4 years, Lexington, Kentucky

I work fifty to fifty-five hours a week, but I take off one week a month and let my support team handle things during that week. The people who enjoy a real estate career the best are those realtors who work in teams or who generate enough income to have a full-time support staff to handle the night and weekend calls.

—Realtor/affiliate broker, 15 years, Charleston, South Carolina

Sixty hours a week, but let's be honest. Is taking a call about a contract issue or a new listing while playing golf or cruising on a houseboat or riding in the Benz really that tough? Hell, I could be installing shingles in 100-degree weather or laying block for a foundation or hundreds of other jobs that are fifty times harder than matching a buyer with a seller.

—Realtor/affiliate broker, 16 years, Sea Island, Georgia

. . .

Have you found advancement within your career easy or difficult?

There are only a few levels of advancement in the real estate world — realtor

to affiliate broker to broker to owner. Each has its pluses and minuses. It depends how independent you want to be and whether earning a percentage of other people's commissions is worth the capital outlay, potential, staff needs, and aggravation.

—Broker, 22 years, Kansas City, Missouri

As a realtor you are an independent contractor. Advancement comes in the form of increased annual income. It is out there for you if you are willing to put in the time.

—Realtor/affiliate broker, 15 years, Richmond, Virginia

I have found it slower than expected. You are in direct competition with so many other agents that have been in business longer and have more listings and more clients. You have to constantly network for potential clients, and the lack of closed sales works against you.

—Realtor, 1 year, Jackson, Mississippi

THE BEST AND THE WORST

What do you spend most of your day doing? Describe a typical day.

Assessing the status of pending contracts, reviewing listings, seeking new listings, showing properties, and talking to other agents and lenders to be sure deals are moving forward.

—Realtor, 8 years, Georgetown, Kentucky

Supervising agents and solving problems. There is no such thing as a typical day; every day is different. You work with every kind of person under the sun, the amount of paperwork is incredible, and it is either so dead you are wishing something would happen *or* it is crazy busy.

—**Real estate broker, 6 years,
North Little Rock, Arkansas**

Talking to the prospects, doing market research, showing property, dealing with mortgage companies, updating my clients on showings, sending emails, and staying on the cell phone.

—**Realtor, 12 years, San Diego, California**

. . .

What are the best parts of your profession?

Helping people achieve the American dream of owning their own home, and then having them send you a referral as thanks for all you did.

—**Realtor, 6 years, Decatur, Alabama**

The ability to work for myself.

—**Realtor, 11 years, Dalton, Georgia**

The freedom to be my own boss and the opportunity to make an excellent living.

—**Real estate broker, 19 years,
Spokane, Washington**

. . .

What are the least enjoyable aspects of your profession?

Having to live check to check without a salary.

—**Realtor, 2 years, Antioch, Tennessee**

People forgetting that we too have personal lives and thinking we should basically be on-call twenty-four hours a day.

—**Realtor, 11 years, Hartford, Connecticut**

Managing people and dealing with their tendency to ignore problems rather than solve them. We are in the people business and problem-solving business.

—**Real estate broker, 17 years,
Eugene, Oregon**

CHANGES IN THE PROFESSION

What changes do you foresee for your profession?

Greater professional educational requirements and more use of technology, including a push to digital documents. The vast use of the internet will continue to impact the profession greatly.

—**Real estate broker, 19 years,
Buffalo, New York**

More cross-training in various skills. They want land people trained in both the development and construction aspects of the industry. They also want their people to have a finance background, instead of using a separate person to do that analysis, as in the past.

**—Private land consultant,
production home builder, 6 years,
Nashville, Tennessee**

Three major things — more technology, faster technology, easier-to-use technology. Yet all this technology will not eliminate the role of the real estate agent. This is still a people business. The technology can give you the latest information, but if problems or concerns arise with the terms of the sale or the finalization of the financing, and they always do, you will need people to negotiate and solve them.

**—Real estate broker, 22 years,
Miami, Florida**

WOULD YOU DO IT ALL OVER AGAIN?

Do you find your daily job fulfilling?

Every day is different. There are some days everything you touch turns to gold, then there are others where the option of walking on broken glass barefoot with anvils being dropped on your head looks appealing.

**—Real estate broker, 8 years,
Greensboro, North Carolina**

Most days yes, especially when working with a first-time home buyer. They appreciate your time so much more and are very appreciative of what all you have done or are doing for them.

—Realtor, 2 years, Spring Hill, Tennessee

Yes; every day brings new challenges and new opportunities.

**—Realtor/affiliate broker, 7 years,
Wilmington, Delaware**

. . .

Would you choose the same profession again?

Yes. You help people fulfill their dreams with what is for most the largest investment of their life. In doing so you meet a host of interesting people from all walks of life.

**—Realtor/affiliate broker, 10 years,
San Antonio, Texas**

Yes. I don't know where you can make as much money with this small of a capital investment. That is not to say that when interest rates shoot up and sales slow down, it is not challenging. You have to take advantage of all your sales opportunities, big or small.

**—Real estate broker, 24 years,
Louisville, Kentucky**

Yes. However, I would have had a minor in finance in college, since in the commercial real estate business, it is as much finance as real estate.

**—Officer in real estate development
company, 31 years, Memphis, Tennessee**

SO YOU WANT TO BE AN INSURANCE AGENT

If you have done it right along the way, the longer you are in this business, the less you should have to work. The best part about the insurance business is the residual income. My goal has always been that once I sign up new customers, I want those customers for life. Every time they pay a premium for their homeowner's or auto insurance, I make money. The more customers I keep, the more I make and the less I have to work each year.

In the simplest terms, working in the field of insurance means assisting businesses and individuals in guarding against loss. To protect against loss, the insurance industry has created a series of products (or policies) that are made available to both companies and individuals at a certain cost (or premium). The business of insurance companies is centered almost entirely on risk management. We are surrounded by risks every day. If we drive a car, we risk getting in an accident. If we own a home, there is the risk that it could be damaged by fire, winds, flood, or other catastrophe. If we own a business, our inventory could be destroyed, or one of our employees could injure him- or herself or someone else, and so on.

Insurance companies employ actuaries to analyze statistical data, such as mortality, accident, sickness, disability, and retirement rates, and they then construct probability tables to forecast risk and liability for payment of future benefits. Calculations are then made to ascertain the premium rates required and cash reserves necessary to ensure payment of future benefits. Different criteria are considered depending on the loss being covered, the risk being managed, and the insurance products being offered to protect against the loss.

The concept of insurance can be traced all the way back to ancient Babylonia, where traders were encouraged to assume the risks of the caravan trade through loans that were repaid (with interest) only after the goods had arrived safely. The Phoenicians and the Greeks applied a similar system to their seaborne commerce. By the middle of the fourteenth century, marine insurance was practically universal among the maritime nations of Europe. In London, in the late 1600s, Lloyd's Coffee House was a place where merchants, shipowners, and underwriters met to transact business. By the end of the eighteenth century, Lloyd's had progressed into one of the first modern insurance companies.

Today, the three most common types of insurance are *property and casualty insurance* (for automobiles, homes, and businesses), *health insurance*, and *life insurance*. To sell these, insurance companies either create their own sales force of insurance brokers and agents or allow independent agents to offer their various insurance products. Agents who work exclusively for one insurance company, offering only their products for sale, such as the neighborhood offices of Allstate or State Farm, are sometimes referred to within the industry as "captive agents." Independent agents offer insurance coverage by a large number of different carriers. Insurance agents are almost exclusively independent contractors, rather than employees of the insurance company or companies they represent.

Brokers and agents are paid a portion of the premiums that the insurers collect. The level of compensation is based upon a series of different formulas that take into consideration the amount of the premiums paid and the length of term that the policy remains in force. Agents receive their income under a variety of compensation arrangements, including straight commission, draws against commission, and salary plus commission. For a productive insurance agent, annual income levels can be quite attractive, especially if old policies stay on the books for a long time, thus providing a source of residual income each year.

Until the 1950s, most insurance companies in the United States were restricted to providing only one type of insurance, but then legislation was passed to allow companies to underwrite several classes of insurance. After that, firms expanded and merged, and multiple-line companies now dominate the field. In 1999, Congress repealed banking laws that had prohibited commercial banks from being in the insurance business, and major banks quickly jumped into the insurance arena.

The distinctions between the banking industry, the investment industry, and the insurance industry are quickly evaporating. This allows major companies to provide a wider range of services to their customers/policyholders. To reflect this, most major insurance companies now refer to themselves as financial groups.

If you're looking to become an insurance agent, this means you are as likely to find a job at your local bank as at your local insurance office. There are no specific academic requirements for entering the field (though you must be licensed in your state), but it helps to have a college degree or background in business and sales. Like all sales positions, selling insurance successfully requires the skills of time management, persuasion, and excellent communication.

No matter how much our modern world changes, there will always be risks, and there will always be a need to help manage the costs of those risks with insurance.

BY THE NUMBERS

EMPLOYMENT LEVELS: According to the U.S. Bureau of Labor Statistics, there are 400,000 insurance agents in the United States, with one in four being self-employed.

ACADEMIC REQUIREMENTS: There are no specific academic requirements for becoming an insurance agent. Many individuals enter the profession after spending time in other careers. Most states require anyone selling insurance products to pass an examination related to those particular types of insurance; thus, agents are required to be separately licensed to sell life insurance and annuities, casualty insurance, property insurance, and health insurance. If agents also offer financial products (such as mutual funds, bonds, and securities), such transactions must be conducted by or in conjunction with someone licensed by their state to sell those products, sometimes referred to as broker-dealers. Most states also require insurance agents to take a minimum annual number of continuing education courses.

AVERAGE SALARY LEVELS: According to the U.S. Bureau of Labor Statistics, the annual median earnings for insurance agents are **$41,720**; the range for annual earnings goes from **$23,170** to **$108,800**.

COLLEGE VS. REALITY

How would you compare the reality of your profession to the picture you had of it while in school?

I did not anticipate going into the field of insurance, so I really didn't have a picture of it in my mind. Insurance sales are just that — sales. Sure, there are a lot of aspects to placing insurance for a customer, and getting a customer approved takes a much greater effort than most customers understand, but being an insurance agent revolves mostly around getting the customer in the first place.

—**Insurance agent, 12 years,**
Wilmington, North Carolina

I took business courses in school, and my family knew people in the insurance business, but until you are actually selling insurance, you don't appreciate that you spend most of your time building a customer base. If you are good with people and are unafraid to approach anyone to talk about their business and personal needs, and if you are not in a hurry to get rich, you can forge a comfortable living selling insurance products.

—**Independent insurance agent, 17 years,**
Youngstown, Ohio

There are different tiers or levels of business sophistication within the insurance industry. You have companies that primarily participate in selling auto insurance to anyone who breathes and can come up with that initial premium payment. You then have the neighborhood insurance offices like the Allstates or the Nationwides, which, based upon good corporate support, are traditionally manned by individuals with a greater level of insurance and business acumen and

provide their customers with a wider array of available products and services in more of a long-term agent-customer relationship.

And then there are the insurance agents that are affiliated with the major life insurance companies, who specialize in complete financial planning for wealthy and successful individuals through the use of life insurance, annuities, disability coverage, long-term care insurance, stocks, bonds, and mutual funds. I was lucky enough to have some college instructors who helped pique my interest in pursuing this last career path.

—**Life insurance agent, 15 years,**
Fairfield, Connecticut

. . .

How would you rate your collegiate and graduate courses in preparing you for your profession on a scale of 1 to 10, with 10 being the best?

A 10. I went to an excellent liberal arts school that taught me how to think and write. My success at work is because I think outside the box. I entered the health insurance business with no formal business education. My textbook was the business my father ran in the small town I grew up in. I began working there when I was thirteen. I learned who the customers were and that they paid the bills. I operate from my gut rather than textbooks.

—Health insurance executive, 20 years,
Chattanooga, Tennessee

The best way to learn about the insurance business would be to do internships, but unlike other careers, the insurance industry does not have the framework that supports learning on the job. Unlike advertising or the legal profession or veterinary medicine, where the clients or patients are already in place and as an intern you can observe and work along the edges, with insurance, it all centers around making a sale. Once the customer is secured, the central issues of approval and underwriting and ultimate premium cost are handled by the insurance company. To make it in insurance sales, you have to take a leap of faith and get out there and find customers. Once that is accomplished, the support framework to close the sale is in place for you to work through.

—Independent insurance broker, 11 years,
Mt. Pleasant, South Carolina

5. Most people who end up in insurance do not plan that career. Many come from other professions, but their skills and personalities are a good fit for sales work. I came from a retail background, working in the family business. I was good with people and had a business administration degree,

so a move into insurance was not a difficult transition.

However, if I had known I was going to end up here, I would have taken more courses directed to financial matters. People are now looking to their insurance agents for more financial advice and answers about financial planning.

—Insurance agent, 5 years,
Cape Girardeau, Missouri

THE BIGGEST SURPRISE

What most surprised you about your chosen profession?

How competitive it is. It is a lot like the real estate profession. There are a lot of people in the industry. The person who is the most successful is the one who can make the relationships from which to develop the largest client base.

—Insurance agent, 8 years, Mobile, Alabama

How much the public still does not understand about insurance. Most people pay an auto policy and/or a homeowner's policy, but when a claim comes about, the ins and outs of the policies and the coverage are completely foreign to them.

—Insurance agent, 6 years,
Nashua, New Hampshire

How much money you can make in this business! It is not handed to you on a platter, but if you work hard and constantly build relationships in your community, the sky is the limit.

—Independent insurance broker, 14 years,
Lyndhurst, Ohio

HOURS AND ADVANCEMENT

How many hours do you work each week at your career?

As an independent contractor owning a neighbor office associated with a national company, I set my own hours. As I work solely on commissions, and no one is paying me a fixed salary, I have to put in whatever time proves necessary to make a decent living. For me that is fifty to fifty-five hours a week.

—Insurance agent, 10 years, Macon, Georgia

I am an independent sales agent. I work for myself. Some weeks I work thirty hours, and some weeks I work sixty hours. It all depends on what it takes to get the work done. If the work doesn't get done, I can't feed my family.

—Independent insurance agent, 16 years,
Chesterfield, Missouri

If you have done it right along the way, the longer you are in this business, the less you should have to work. The best part about the insurance business is the residual income. My goal has always been that once I sign up new customers,

I want those customers for life. Every time they pay a premium for their homeowner's or auto insurance, I make money. The more customers I keep, the more I make and the less I have to work each year.

—Independent insurance agent, 11 years,
Milwaukee, Wisconsin

. . .

Have you found advancement within your career easy or difficult?

Unlike in other professions, there is no set path for advancement. You are in control of your own rate of advancement, which is one of the benefits of being in insurance that attracted me. I work for myself, and if I work hard and smart, I should make more money.

—Insurance agent, 8 years,
Gainesville, Florida

Unless you plan to go into the management side or work in corporate for one of the major companies, advancement in the world of insurance sales means writing more business. It is that simple.

—Life insurance agent, 12 years,
Lancaster, Pennsylvania

If you are an insurance agent, your advancement is based upon the number of policies you write, which is based on the number of customers you have.

There are no inside politics that you have to navigate, no one's ass that you have to particularly kiss.

If you can put up with all the hoops regarding risk assessment and underwriting that you have to jump through to get new customers insured, the sky is the limit. There are millions of people out there, and they all need insurance of one form or another.

—**Independent insurance broker, 17 years, Jackson, Mississippi**

THE BEST AND THE WORST

What do you spend most of your day doing? Describe a typical day.

As the co-owner of a local independent insurance agency, I typically spend my days seeking new business, talking with the underwriting departments of the many major carriers where I can place coverage, and being sure my staff is keeping up with the constant stream of support data and paperwork that back up the steps we have taken to insure our customers.

—**Independent insurance agent, 13 years, Alexandria, Virginia**

There never is a typical day. Hopefully the seeds you have gradually planted in the community will cause your phone to ring, which can be the start to a relationship that leads to a new customer

and a new revenue stream. My goal is to get one new customer a day.

—**Insurance agency owner, 4 years, Brentwood, Tennessee**

My days are filled with a variety of activities, all of which are centered around the same goal of matching the needs of my clients with the right mix of insurance and financial products. That can mean that I am spending time meeting with a client to secure the necessary level of information from which to intelligently proceed, or working with the home office to secure the approval of the coverage, or talking with my company's broker-dealers. The goal is to get the complete package of products for each client's financial plan finalized and activated. At times, getting it right can be a long and laborious process, but income benefits to me have over the years made it worthwhile.

—**Life insurance agent/certified financial planner, 26 years, Tampa, Florida**

. . .

What are the best parts of your profession?

We are in the people business. If you cannot get some satisfaction from assisting your customers with their needs, you need to find a different line of work.

—**Insurance agent, 19 years, Annapolis, Maryland**

My background is life insurance and estate planning. In addition to making a generous living, I am afforded the satisfaction of matching my talents to the needs of my clients, so that their families' futures are more secure, and they can concentrate on doing what they do best in their own business or industry.

—Life insurance agent/chartered financial consultant, 24 years, Chicago, Illinois

Making relationships with people who start out as customers and end up as friends.

—Insurance agent, 15 years, Shreveport, Louisiana

. . .

What are the least enjoyable aspects of your profession?

The procedures that you have to go through to get someone approved for insurance. Insurance is a highly regulated industry with a lot of internal guidelines that must be followed. My best asset is being able to quickly make relationships with potential customers.

—Insurance agent, 7 years, Paducah, Kentucky

For me it is having to overcome the general public's preconceptions about insurance salesmen. In some people's eyes, insurance salesmen are just a step above car salesmen. But it is like most professions; there are people who just want to make a sale, and to hell with the customer service if a claim results, and then there are people who want to build long-term relationships to meet the expanding needs of people or their businesses as their lives get more complicated.

—Insurance agent, 3 years, Anderson, Indiana

Having to deal with the emotions of a family that has experienced a tragic accident or a death. Money and emotions rarely mix well.

—Independent insurance agent, 18 years, McAllen, Texas

CHANGES IN THE PROFESSION

What changes do you foresee for your profession?

The consumer will be offered the opportunity to purchase insurance in more locations, such as his or her bank. Consumers will have to decide if price is the key factor, or if they desire to maintain a more personal relationship with someone who specializes just in the insurance industry.

—Insurance agent, 9 years, Huntsville, Alabama

Technology will continue to change the insurance industry. It is really a double-edged sword. Technology has allowed insurance agents to greatly reduce the amount of paperwork, thus allowing us to keep better track of more customers. But at the same time, the internet has caused a major shift in how consumers purchase insurance products. Many policies, especially with auto insurance, are handled by companies directly, eliminating the need to interact with an agent.

—Insurance agent, 15 years, Boise, Idaho

The need for insurance agents, especially multiline agents, to participate in more continuing education. Banks are getting into the insurance business big-time, and if you want to retain your customers and attract new ones, you will have to be knowledgeable about a wider range of products, especially financial ones.

—Independent insurance agent, 8 years, Myrtle Beach, South Carolina

WOULD YOU DO IT ALL OVER AGAIN?

Do you find your daily job fulfilling?

Yes. I have been in the insurance business for over twenty years and have built up a wonderful support staff. This allows me to spend a good part of my day staying involved in the business and social circles of my community, building relationships that can lead to future business.

—Independent insurance agency owner, 24 years, Cleveland, Tennessee

Not really. I spend most of my days trying to sell life insurance to business owners. I would prefer to spend my days actually running my own small business where people come into my store for products or services. As a life insurance agent, I can't seem to distinguish myself from the others in my field, the way I know I could with my own retail or service business.

—Insurance agent, 8 years, Bloomington, Indiana

The insurance business has afforded me a nice lifestyle. It is not the perfect career, but it is one that you can prosper in because everyone has some risk or loss they need to avoid or minimize. If I had to do it all over again, I see myself back in this same people-oriented, sales profession.

—Independent insurance agent, 18 years, Kalamazoo, Michigan

. . .

Would you choose the same profession again?

I am relatively new to the insurance business, and the worst part for me was figuring out which products I could best sell so that I was using my time most efficiently. It took me a while, but I realized that concentrating on life insurance sales was not for me. I did much better concentrating on the more bread-and-butter products like home and auto. Now that I have worked through that self-adjustment period, I would choose this profession again.

—Insurance agent, 3 years, Tigard, Oregon

Yes. There are not many careers where you can plant seeds in one year and have them keep bearing fruit for twenty or more years. Residuals are great!

—Independent insurance agent, 17 years, Little Rock, Arkansas

Insurance sales afford you the opportunity to have a financially productive career if you are not cut out for medical school or law school or do not have an aptitude for engineering. You don't have to be brilliant, but you do have to be bright. If you want to handle some of the affairs of very successful people, you will have to have a sound grasp of business issues, get it right the first time, and be responsive to the needs of your customer base.

—Life insurance agent, 12 years, Bellevue, Washington

CAREERS IN

Geoscience

SO YOU WANT TO BE A GEOLOGIST

Most people think in terms of the petroleum or mining industries, or working for a governmental agency, but with a master's you can, among other things, end up studying the ocean floor, ocean basins, and continental shelves as a marine geologist, the evolution of the solar system as a planetary geologist, or the movement of glaciers and ice sheets as a glacial geologist. Your life as a geologist can be as mundane or as unique as you allow it to be.

Geology is the scientific study of the origin, history, and structure of the earth — its composition and processes. The word "geology" is derived from two Greek words — *ge* (earth) and *logos* (knowledge). Geologists help locate and manage the earth's natural resources, including oil, natural gas, coal, metals (such as iron, copper, and uranium), gemstones, and minerals (such as mica, quartz, phosphate, and silica). Also, in a world increasingly threatened by industry and overpopulation, geologists are integral players in monitoring the earth's environment.

Basic geological concepts concerning the origin of the earth date back to ancient Greece. The word "geology" was first used in 1778, as the growth of the eighteenth-century's mining industry created an economic motivation for systematic and detailed studies of the composition of the earth's strata. Charles Lyell published *Principles of Geology* in 1830. During the nineteenth century, Canada, Australia, Great Britain, and the United States funded geological surveys that produced geological maps of vast areas of the globe. The stratigraphical column was also developed in the nineteenth century; this was significant because it provided a method for assigning a relative age to rocks by slotting them into different positions in their stratigraphical sequence. This helped bring consistency to geological dating of the earth (which, incidentally, is considered about 4.6 billion years old). Geologists developed the theory of continental drift in the early twentieth century, which was replaced in the 1960s by the current concept of plate tectonics.

Today, geology uses an increasingly integrative approach that encompasses all the earth's processes, including those of the atmosphere, biosphere, and hydrosphere. Satellite photography has fostered and allowed for this, and satellite images have improved geological mapping, pinpointing the location of natural resources, and the prediction of natural disasters caused by plate shifts.

Most geologists work either for business or for the government in a regulatory capacity; pure scientific research is less common. *Petroleum geologists* map the subsurface of the oceans and the land in the search for oil and gas deposits; as known reserves shrink, this is becoming ever more vital. *Engineering geologists* focus on civil and environmental engineering, offering advice on major construction projects and assisting in environmental remediation and hazard reduction. *Glacial geologists* study and interpret the impact from the movement of glaciers and ice sheets, which is occurring at levels never seen before. *Seismological geologists* interpret data from seismographs and other geophysical instruments to study (and hopefully predict) earthquakes and tsunamis in hopes of saving lives around the world.

Some geologists work for state and federal agencies conducting research and mapping activities, while other government-employed geologists work for various regulatory bodies, which monitor mining and other industries that threaten our environment with leaks and hazards.

Over a hundred colleges offer either a four- or five-year bachelor's degree in the geosciences. Many geologists elect to complete a master's program before entering the workforce. Unlike with engineering, which requires up to five years of engineering work experience before one can become a "professional engineer," you can become a "professional geologist" (PG), and thus sign off on official remediation and other geological reports, without first completing years of field experience.

Persons who like working outside, doing field research, and working as part of a team may want to consider geoscience as a career. Geologists work on a regular basis with other professionals, such as engineers, chemists, and soil scientists. As a general distinction, soil scientists concentrate on the surface of the earth (to a depth of about six feet), while geologists study the whole earth, concentrating on data from below six feet.

Course study includes, among others things, physical geology, mineralogy, petrology, paleontology, geochemistry, and hydro-geology. Good math skills and computer skills are essential, as geologists now use computer modeling and digital mapping, along with GIS (Global Information System) and GPS (Global Positioning System) technology on a regular basis.

BY THE NUMBERS

EMPLOYMENT LEVELS: According to the U.S. Bureau of Labor Statistics, there are approximately 30,000 geologists employed in the United States. However, if you incorporate all of the professions that fall under geoscience (such as geomorphology, geophysics, hydro-geology, marine geology, planetary geology, and volcanology), the number jumps to over 100,000, according to the National Science Foundation.

ACADEMIC REQUIREMENTS: A bachelor's degree in geology or the geosciences is required. Many graduates elect to complete a master's degree with a specialty in one phase of the geosciences. Twenty-eight states now register and license geologists. To become licensed in those states, graduates must pass a national examination on the fundamentals and practice of geology, which was developed and is administered by the National Association of State Boards of Geology (ASBOG).

AVERAGE SALARY LEVELS: According to the U.S. Bureau of Labor Statistics, the annual median earnings for geoscientists are **$68,730;** the range of annual earnings is from **$37,700** to **$130,750.** Those working for the government traditionally receive lower salaries than those employed in the private sector or those who maintain their own consulting firms.

COLLEGE VS. REALITY

How would you compare the reality of your profession to the picture you had of it while in school?

My picture of the profession was in broad terms brought on by the academia of college — involvement in predicting the behavior of the earth and balancing the world's demand for natural resources with somehow sustaining healthy ecosystems. The reality is a much more narrow and capitalism-driven profession, where companies use geologists in a monitoring position to respond to ever-increasing environmental regulations.

—Engineering geologist, 10 years,
Tucker, Georgia

I understood what I was going to be doing, but I did not fully appreciate the level of reliance by others on my work product. As a professional geologist you have signatory authority for submission of data to governmental regulatory agencies. In school you only have a textbook concept of this reality.

—**Professional geologist, 5 years, Hoover, Alabama**

The reality of being a geologist centers around the willingness to do the fieldwork on which larger decisions are based. Until you are involved in gathering groundwater samples or results from monitoring wells or acquiring data that allow you to monitor the quality of air emissions, you can't properly picture the daily life of a field geologist.

—**Professional geologist, 7 years, Missoula, Montana**

. . .

How would you rate your collegiate and graduate courses in preparing you for your profession on a scale of 1 to 10, with 10 being the best?

A 5. Until you have extensive hands-on fieldwork in both investigatory and remedial projects, the work of being a geologist remains rather abstract.

—**Engineering geologist, 3 years, Oklahoma City, Oklahoma**

A 6.

—**Petroleum geologist, 12 years, Houston, Texas**

From a science background, a 9. From a practical standpoint, a 4. There should be much more fieldwork. Required internships would be a plus.

—**Hydro-geologist, 4 years, Tucson, Arizona**

THE BIGGEST SURPRISE

What most surprised you about your chosen profession?

How many other decisions your data impact. With a remedial project, for example, your involvement can be at the center of whether fines or work stoppages are issued.

—**Government geologist, 2 years, Charleston, West Virginia**

How many different directions you could go with a geology background. Most people think in terms of the petroleum or mining industries, or working for a governmental agency, but with a master's you can, among other things, end up studying the ocean floor, ocean basins, and continental shelves as a marine geologist, the evolution of the solar system as a planetary geologist, or the movement of glaciers and ice sheets as a glacial geologist. Your life as a geologist can be as mundane or unique as you allow it to be.

—**Marine geologist, 6 years, New Orleans, Louisiana**

The difficulty in retaining a love for fieldwork and still increasing your income levels within the profession. Historically, the best bet for the highest paid fieldwork is in the oil industry.

—Petroleum geologist, 16 years,
Beaumont, Texas

HOURS AND ADVANCEMENT

How many hours do you work each week at your career?

It is dependent on the needs of our clients. It can vary from forty to fifty per week. If you factor in travel time, it can be much more.

—Professional geologist, 7 years,
Denver, Colorado

It varies from month to month. I can have project needs that require me to do field testing for one to two straight weeks. Then there are other times that I am in the office in a more normal eight-to-five setting. It probably averages out to about fifty hours a week.

—Engineering geologist, 11 years,
Fort Collins, Colorado

When I was doing exclusively fieldwork associated with remediation work, my days could run twelve hours. Now, as a project manager, I find my days more predictable — eight to ten hours a day.

—Professional geologist, 15 years,
Las Vegas, Nevada

. . .

Have you found advancement within your career easy or difficult?

The largest employer of geoscientists has historically been the petroleum industry. Job opportunities or the lack thereof in the petroleum industry has in turn been directly related to oil prices. Now that they are at record levels, exploration for new sources of energy will allow for more jobs, better salaries, and advancement on a professionwide level.

—Petroleum geologist, 8 years,
Houston, Texas

If you work for a comprehensive environmental firm, advancement usually means moving out of fieldwork and into project management. If your firm keeps growing and attracting more business, opportunities are usually there for those who want them.

—Professional geologist, 11 years,
Salt Lake City, Utah

As a member of an international, seven-hundred-man comprehensive environment firm, I have found advancement to be dictated by my own ability to inject myself into ongoing projects based upon my expertise and reputation for reliable fieldwork.

—Professional geologist, 12 years,
Brentwood, Tennessee

THE BEST AND THE WORST

What do you spend most of your day doing? Describe a typical day.

My day as a field geologist can consist of collecting and monitoring well data, collaborating with drilling engineers based on developed models, presenting geological reports, and conferring with other professionals, including soil scientists, geochemists, hydrologists, and environmental engineers.

—**Professional geologist, 8 years, Fort Collins, Colorado**

My days as a government geologist are spent investigating mining, industrial, or chemical sites for possible violations of environmental regulations. I am not the most popular guy in the neighborhood.

—**Government geologist, 18 years, Sacramento, California**

As a project supervisor, I review data generated from the field geologists working under me on any particular project. That can include such things as geological risk analyses of certain industrial activities, remediation associated with the removal of aged pipeline, or verifying compliance by retail gas station sites involving tank integrity.

—**Engineering geologist, 14 years, Dallas, Texas**

. . .

What are the best parts of your profession?

The opportunities to use my scientific knowledge to make a difference in the world. Geologists are the ones who will have the most direct input in how we will continue to provide energy sources for an exploding world population.

—**Petroleum geologist, 9 years, Houston, Texas**

Being able to practice my knowledge of science within a framework that is considerate of the fragility of our environment.

—**Seismological geologist, 6 years, San Diego, California**

Being outside most of the day and not having to be one of the "suits," and yet still being able to be a practicing scientist.

—**Marine geologist, 12 years, Miami, Florida**

. . .

What are the least enjoyable aspects of your profession?

The travel. When you are single, the travel to different states is rather enjoyable. But once you have a family, it gets old pretty quick. Of course, it depends where you live, but generally most investigative and remediation work takes you to locations where large industrial

217

sites, refineries, pipeline, energy plants, and the like are located, and you can be gone a week or two at a time.

—**Professional geologist, 8 years,**
Boulder, Colorado

The lack of understanding by most people as to what we do as geologists. The general public and even many professionals do not appreciate the direct connection between their energy needs or their environmental concerns and geology as a science.

—**Petroleum geologist, 4 years,**
Midland, Texas

The view by the private world of engineering and even the governmental agencies that geology is a subscience. While that view is gradually changing with a more environmentally conscious world, municipal and state budgets do not prioritize monitoring positions. In the private sector, it is rare to see a geologist at the top levels of a multi-discipline engineering firm.

—**Engineering geologist, 17 years,**
Chestnut Hill, Massachusetts

CHANGES IN THE PROFESSION

What changes do you foresee for your profession?

The role of geoscience moving more to the forefront as concerns about global warming and rising sea levels increase worldwide.

—**Glacial geologist, 7 years,**
Washington, D.C.

A better appreciation for the expertise of geoscientists in monitoring, investigative, and remediation roles as governmental bodies at all levels increase their environmental regulations.

—**Government geologist, 15 years,**
Portland, Oregon

As the known deposits of oil reserves are consumed at a frightening pace, the pressure on the petroleum industry to find new reserves will intensify to an almost desperate pitch. Geologists will be at the heart of any solution.

—**Petroleum geologist, 12 years,**
Dallas, Texas

WOULD YOU DO IT ALL OVER AGAIN?

Do you find your daily job fulfilling?

Initially I did, when I had the opportunity to travel to remote locations in the world looking for oil reserves. But after years of fieldwork in dangerous conditions, which I once found challenging and even exhilarating, I am ready to give this aspect of the profession over to a younger geologist.

—**Petroleum geologist, 19 years,**
Arlington, Texas

As a young geologist, I find my profession to be increasingly pivotal as we try to balance the worldwide need for energy with an attempt to save our planet.

—**Marine geologist, 3 years,
Corpus Christi, Texas**

As the ecosystem balance of the world seems to be getting more out of sync, I view my work monitoring geological changes in the earth as even more critical as we improve our ability to more accurately predict tsunamis and install a better warning system.

—**Seismological geologist, 10 years,
Menlo Park, California**

. . .

Would you choose the same profession again?

Yes. However, I would stay in school longer in an effort to concentrate on glacial activity and ice sheet shrinkage, which would be a more timely focus.

—**Professional geologist, 14 years,
Redmond, Washington**

No. I would go into more mainstream engineering, which allows for a lifestyle that is more predictable and permits you to market your skills to a broader client base.

—**Professional geologist, 9 years,
Reston, Virginia**

Yes. I love research and on-site data collection. I am not someone who would be happy inside a skyscraper somewhere.

—**Engineering geologist, 7 years,
Ft. Collins, Colorado**

SO YOU WANT TO BE A
SOIL SCIENTIST

The role of the soil scientist is becoming more important with increasing amounts of land being converted to development and an increasing awareness of the necessity to conserve our land and protect our soils, water, and other natural resources. There will be an even greater demand for information regarding all our natural resources as time goes on.

Though we rarely stop to consider it, our lives depend almost entirely on the quality of our soil. Soils are the resource for all plants, and in turn for our food, but they also support our buildings and are the medium for waste disposal. They distribute and store water and other nutrients that are critical to our environment. Historically speaking, the distribution and quality of soil have influenced the worldwide distribution of plants, animals, and people. And with greater strains being put on the earth today, the role of the soil scientist is becoming increasingly important.

Some have always appreciated the critical importance of soil. Thomas Jefferson once stated, "Civilization itself rests upon the soil," and Mahatma Gandhi cautioned, "To forget how to tend the soil is to forget ourselves." In a time when our planet is experiencing the most dramatic climatic changes in thousands of years, including the erosion of major portions of the world's tillable soil, Jefferson's and Gandhi's words were clearly prophetic.

But what is soil exactly?

In one early concept of soil, German chemist Justus von Liebig (1803–1873) considered soil more or less a static storage bin for plant nutrients. This led to a balance-sheet theory of plant nutrition — plants took nutrients from the soil, and nutrients were returned through manure, lime, and fertilizer. Geologists describe soil as disintegrated rock of various sorts — granite, sandstone, glacial till, and others — that were shaped into landforms, such as glacier moraines, alluvial plains, loess plains, and marine terraces.

Beginning in 1870, Russian V. V. Dokuchaev helped establish the study of soil as a natural science; he suggested soil was a natural body having its own genesis, a body with complex and multiform processes taking place within it, each type resulting from a unique combination of climate, living matter, parent material, relief, and time. In the 1930s, C. F. Marbut adapted this concept to conditions in the United States, and he emphasized that classification of soils should be based on morphology (the study of the form and structure of organisms as a whole) rather than on theories of soil genesis. Most studies of the soil at this time were aimed at improving crop yield predictions.

In the 1950s and 1960s, nonfarm uses of soil were increasing. The U.S. government, to better meet the needs of both the agricultural and nonagricultural users of soils, created a new soil classification system under the direction of Guy Smith, who in 1975 published *Soil Taxonomy: A Basis System of Soil Classification for Making and Interpreting Soil Surveys*. The Smith system has since formed the basis of classification systems worldwide.

Today, soil science has evolved into the environmental science of dealing with soils as a natural resource. It involves studying soil formation, classification, and mapping; understanding the physical, chemical, biological, and fertility properties of soils; and studying the human use and management of soils (such as soil conservation, land use, water quality, and waste management issues). The job of a soil scientist includes *collection of soil data*, *consultation*, *investigation*, *evaluation*, *interpretation*, *planning*, and *inspection*. Soil types are complex, and soil scientists work in every conceivable geographical area.

To excel as a soil scientist, you should have good observation skills, like science and math, prefer to work outside, and want to be a part of environmental studies and decision making. To pursue a career, you need a bachelor's degree in soil science, which involves studying soil biology, soil chemistry, soil classification, soil morphology, mapping, soil conservation and management, soil fertility, and soil physics. Many soil scientists find employment with some type of government agency — such as the National Resource Conservation System, a state natural resources agency, a national or state board of health, and county conservation organizations. They also work in the private sector, possibly as a wetland specialist, a hydrologist, or a soil- or water-quality specialist within a multidiscipline engineering firm.

Soil scientists can also become certified as "professional soil scientists" and establish their own consulting businesses, offering their services to developers, builders, homeowners, farmers, engineers, and architects. To qualify for certification, soil scientists must pass a series of national exams on soil science, and to qualify to take the exams, they must have several years of work experience in the field under the supervision of a professional soil scientist.

BY THE NUMBERS

EMPLOYMENT LEVELS: According to the U.S. Bureau of Labor Statistics, there are 32,000 individuals employed as conservation scientists, which includes soil scientists and foresters. One in three works for the federal government.

ACADEMIC REQUIREMENTS: A bachelor's degree in soil science is required to work as a soil scientist. Graduates must work under the supervision of professional soil scientists for several years (the exact amount varies from state to state), and then they can take a series of national tests to become licensed themselves as professional soil scientists.

AVERAGE SALARY LEVELS: According to the U.S. Bureau of Labor Statistics, the annual median earnings for conservation scientists are **$52,480**; the range of annual earnings is from **$30,740** to **$78,470**. In 2007 CNN Money reported that the average salary for a soil scientist in the United States was **$58,723**. Traditionally, the private sector pays more than government positions at the starting levels.

COLLEGE VS. REALITY

How would you compare the reality of your profession to the picture you had of it while in school?

As regards the fieldwork, it is much like I anticipated, because as part of college we participated with faculty in fieldwork on many weekends.

—**Soil scientist, 3 years, Cedar Rapids, Iowa**

I had a pretty good idea about the overview of the job, but I greatly underestimated the politics and the bureaucracy that come when one works for or is affiliated with a government agency, especially when one is the new kid on the block.

—**Soil scientist, 2 years, Lawrence, Kansas**

I understood when I graduated what was expected of me as a soil scientist. What I did not fully appreciate was how, in the private sector, you are part of a much larger team, and there are definitely chains of command. In the scope of a large engineering firm, when you factor soil scientists in with engineers, landscape architects, and surveyors, we are at the bottom of the food chain.

—Soil scientist, 5 years, Decatur, Georgia

. . .

How would you rate your collegiate and graduate courses in preparing you for your profession on a scale of 1 to 10, with 10 being the best?

From the perspective of what is expected of me as far as my knowledge of soils and the environment is concerned, I would rate it about an 8 or 9.

—Soil scientist, 2 years, Frankfort, Kentucky

I left college with a very good physiographic and geomorphic background.

—Soil scientist, 8 years, Austin, Texas

If you take full advantage of the courses that are available, you can leave college with an excellent understanding of the science of soil and its critical importance in our environment. The key is in your ability to translate your knowledge into good interpretative, evaluative, investigatory skills and then be able to communicate the results to a cross section of different people in a variety of different life and business settings. You only learn that from actually doing it on a daily basis.

—Soil scientist, 4 years, Knoxville, Tennessee

THE BIGGEST SURPRISE

What most surprised you about your chosen profession?

How little the average person knows about the soils and their overall importance, and how few women are in the profession.

—Soil scientist, 2 years, Roanoke, Virginia

The fact that some very intelligent professionals — engineers, architects, and commercial contractors — do not place more importance on the geomorphology of the soils of their large construction projects.

—Soil scientist, 11 years,
Wheaton, Maryland

The level of fiscal charades when it comes to the way the federal government handles its funding of the budget that relates to issues within the domain of soil conservation. For example, after Katrina, many of the states and counties pushed for federal dollars for agricultural cleanup and reassessment. The prior mapping of much of the area in the gulf states became obsolete in a matter of days when soils at great depths were dramatically rearranged. Yet funds that were approved for use in these drastically affected areas ended up being used on more localized projects and internal budgets as directed by district conservationists in concert with local politicians.

—Soil scientist, 6 years, Jackson, Mississippi

HOURS AND ADVANCEMENT

How many hours do you work each week at your career?

It varies, but at least forty to forty-five.
—Soil scientist, 12 years, Savannah, Georgia

It can depend on how much soil mapping I have to accomplish, and on the cooperation of the weather.
—Soil scientist, 4 years, Augusta, Georgia

As a private soil consultant, I base my schedule on how many projects I am working on at one time and the size of the projects. If the developer has platted a fifty-lot subdivision where sewer is not available and septic systems are required, he cannot sell any of those lots until a soil scientist has completed a percolation test on the soils of each lot. Also, the soil will determine how large of a home can be built upon that site, as the number of bedrooms are used as a gauge for occupancy, which in turn dictates the level of usage on the private septic systems.
—Soil scientist, 17 years, Memphis, Tennessee

. . .

Have you found advancement within your career easy or difficult?

If you work for the Natural Resources Conservation Service, there are advancement opportunities, as many of the soil scientists and district conservationists are approaching retirement. However, there are a lot of politics in maneuvering your way to advancement.
—Soil scientist, 8 years, Topeka, Kansas

Soil science does not have the respect of the private marketplace, so advancement can best be found within a governmental agency or district office. Plus the governmental benefits usually are superior to those in the private sector, and once you are hired and secure enough experience to take and then pass your licensing exam, it is very difficult to be fired. However, with the huge government deficit, I anticipate that budgets will remain tight for quite some time.
—Soil scientist, 11 years, Metairie, Louisiana

I have found that advancement is best achieved by doing work on the side as a licensed soil scientist. You can maintain your regular government job and on the weekends do percolation and soil testing for developers and end up with an excellent annual income.
—Soil scientist, 15 years, Rome, Georgia

THE BEST AND THE WORST

What do you spend most of your day doing? Describe a typical day.

How my day is spent is dependent upon the prioritization of my superiors within the multidiscipline engineering firm I work for. My daily work may consist of obtaining soil samples for soil analysis and profiling; meeting with geologists to discuss the geomorphology of a future development site, or with engineers to discuss the compaction of certain soils, or with landscape architects to discuss the drainage aspects and patterns of a site; or producing maps and soil reports for submission to a client or as part of a report to be presented to a regulatory body on behalf of a project.

—Soil scientist, 7 years,
Charlotte, North Carolina

My days are different. One day may consist of running transects and using the auger to collect soil samples all day in the blazing sun under hot, humid conditions, while another may consist of staying in the office all day working toward satisfying my quarterly mapping requirements with the help of the field data I have produced. Another may be spent meeting with local land-owners to advise them on soil or crop rotation or drainage issues.

—Soil scientist, 4 years,
Little Rock, Arkansas

. . .

What are the best parts of your profession?

Applying my love for science in a very practical way that can help others on an individual basis as regards their future homesite or their farmland.

—Soil scientist, 5 years, Lafayette, Indiana

Not being stuck behind a desk every day.

—Soil scientist, 16 years,
Joplin, Missouri

Working outside in nature and doing my part to help others make smart environmental choices.

—Soil scientist, 8 years, Cheyenne, Wyoming

. . .

What are the least enjoyable aspects of your profession?

At times it can be exhausting work using an auger all day long while analyzing the composition, absorption, and permeability of soils.

—Soil scientist, 3 years,
Hattiesburg, Mississippi

The politics — office politics, county politics, district politics, and federal politics. It is a damn wonder anything gets accomplished.

—Soil scientist, 11 years, Dublin, Ohio

The lack of respect that we as soil scientists receive. The public has no comprehension of the degree of science that is at the heart of all that we do.

—Soil scientist, 7 years,
South Bend, Indiana

CHANGES IN THE PROFESSION

What changes do you foresee for your profession?

The role of the soil scientist is becoming more important with increasing amounts of land being converted to development and an increasing awareness of the necessity to conserve our land and protect our soils, water, and other natural resources. There will be an even greater demand for information regarding all our natural resources as time goes on.

—Soil scientist, 5 years, Huntsville, Alabama

Mapping of urban and metropolitan areas — and not just agricultural and raw land available to be developed — will gradually become the norm in an effort to better assess anthropogenic changes.

—Soil scientist, 12 years, Frederick, Maryland

The use of more technology by soil scientists on a day-to-day basis, through the incorporation and interconnection of GPS [Global Positioning System], GIS [Global Information System], stereoscopic [3D] imaging, and ArcView software.

—Soil scientist, 11 years, Boise, Idaho

WOULD YOU DO IT ALL OVER AGAIN?

Do you find your daily job fulfilling?

I am able to wear blue jeans and drive a truck and yet at the same time utilize the latest GIS and GPS technology. It is a good blend of enjoying your job on a daily basis and yet being sufficiently challenged to keep your interest in science fresh.

—Soil scientist, 5 years, Wilkes-Barre, Pennsylvania

It is about a 5 out of 10. We don't get the respect or pay we deserve for the level of knowledge that we possess, but day to day the job is not bad.

—Soil scientist, 14 years, Bowling Green, Kentucky

I love my job because of the mixture of science and environment issues. I would find it more fulfilling if there were not so many people in the profession who are simply waiting for retirement and cashing a paycheck.

—Soil scientist, 4 years, St. Joseph, Missouri

. . .

Would you choose the same profession again?

There is something about working in nature that calms me, seeing the sunlight shoot through the trees. To be alone in the woods and fields with just the animals is soothing to my soul. I think of all the people in skyscrapers, on subways, stuck on interstates, and I realize that I made the right choice for my career.

**—Soil scientist, 7 years,
Fayetteville, North Carolina**

No. I would pursue landscape architecture instead. Similar time to achieve a degree, and better money.

**—Soil scientist, 11 years,
Kirkland, Washington**

I can be a part of the environment and yet have the academic background and work experience to fully appreciate the interrelationship between the daily choices we make on this planet and their repercussions on the one earth we have. My knowledge of soils gives me an opportunity to advise others to take actions that best impact future generations.

—Soil scientist, 5 years, Springfield, Oregon

CAREERS IN

The Arts and Media

SO YOU WANT TO BE A TELEVISION BROADCASTER

The role of the television broadcaster is rapidly changing because there will be more use of the internet as a way to both acquire information for stories and deliver news to the audience. The traditional delivery of news at six and eleven will gradually morph into more of a menu-type delivery, where the audience can pick and choose what stories it wishes to see, and when.

Up until about five years ago, broadcast journalists were the faces that brought us the news of the world. We would tune in to a morning show before work, the six o'clock newscast after work, and sometimes also the ten or eleven o'clock news before bed to keep up with the events of the day. Sometimes, our favorite broadcast personalities came to feel like part of the family.

But the days of getting our daily news primarily from TV and newspapers is nearly over. An ever-larger percentage of Americans now get their news, at least in part, from the internet. Online, people can select the stories that interest them from a wide array of choices (in such categories as "In the News," "Video Headlines," "Sports," "Shopping," "Strange News," "Community Forums," and more), and online news is constantly updated, so that we can track stories hour by hour if we wish. With the constant stream of information now available online, the merger of our computers and our televisions is getting closer, and it may not be long before televisions and computers are one and the same. Whether the screen is in our living room or on our laptop, we will be able to access the stories we want online, instead of waiting to watch a newscast at a designated time.

Faced with the competition from internet news sites, TV stations across the country are creating their own elaborate websites, with their own up-to-the-minute webcasts with breaking news. Many local stations even offer the ability to receive text message updates on such daily community issues as school closings. In part, these changes are being driven by advertising dollars. With more people turning to the internet for their daily news, advertisers want to be seen where the audience is, and that now means online as well as on-air.

What does this rapidly changing news media landscape mean for those who want to be TV broadcasters and correspondents? In terms of education, aspiring broadcasters still are best served by getting a degree in broadcast journalism or communication, though there are no specific industry requirements to becoming a broadcaster.

You also still need all the skills of a good journalist. You need to be someone who can quickly assess information and prioritize its importance and impact, and who can work well under pressure, since you will be constantly having to meet short on-air deadlines. A curious, investigative mind, research skills, and accuracy are also essential. You should be a good writer and understand the news industry generally — media production, communication, and dissemination. And, of course, you should develop a pleasing on-air personality, one that's confident in delivery and appearance.

Compared to most industries in the United States, television broadcasting offers limited employment opportunities, particularly for on-air positions. To a large degree this is dictated by the fact that there are only 210 "designated market areas" (DMA). A DMA is a region where the population can receive the same television station offerings. Markets are identified by the largest city, which is usually located in the center of the region. Each DMA consists of those counties whose largest share of viewing is of stations located in the same market area. DMAs are used to identify specific media markets for those interested in buying and selling television advertising and programming. With only 210 television markets, on-air personalities traditionally must start working for lower wages in the smallest markets and over a period of years attempt to work their way into larger markets, where salaries are considerably better. During this slow progression, which requires frequent uprooting and relocation, a large percentage of broadcasters leave the business in search of a less glamorous but more stable lifestyle.

What is expected of correspondents is changing, too. With shrinking advertising revenues and shrinking budgets, even television stations in the largest markets are downsizing their news and sports departments (while adding new positions like webmasters and in-house bloggers). Reporters and broadcasters are increasingly being asked to perform "one-man-band" reporting (which was once done only in smaller markets). Rather than always sending a separate camera crew to accompany a reporter to film a news segment, stations are now often asking the broadcast correspondent to handle everything: interview the subject, do the voice-over (VO) or add "sound on tape" (SOT) later, and edit the story in the final form that will appear on the air. The most highly prized news broadcasters are the ones who have already developed all these skills.

Of course, in our information age, there will always be news, and always a need for someone to gather and tell that news. But as an industry, broadcast television is swiftly evolving as technological advances change the way we satisfy our insatiable desire to know what's going on.

BY THE NUMBERS

EMPLOYMENT LEVELS: According to the U.S. Bureau of Labor Statistics, there are 39,000 "announcers" in the United States. This broad category includes all radio, television, freelance, and part-time announcers (which represent 30 percent of this total). There is no individual breakdown of just on-air anchors or broadcasters. However, the United States has a total of 6,000 "broadcast analysts," which includes news analysts, weathercasters, and sportscasters.

ACADEMIC REQUIREMENTS: There are no academic requirements for becoming a television broadcaster, but one is expected to earn a degree in broadcast journalism or communication and to complete as many internships as possible. With only 210 designated market areas (DMAs) in the United States, the competition to become the next Katie Couric, Brian Williams, or Bob Costas is intense.

AVERAGE SALARY LEVELS: Starting salaries are very low in television broadcasting. Traditionally, broadcasters start in a small media market and work their way up (sometimes over many years); the larger the market, the greater the salary. Starting salaries in the smallest markets can be in the **$20,000s**; in the top-ten media markets, anchors can make **SEVEN-FIGURE SALARIES**.

COLLEGE VS. REALITY

How would you compare the reality of your profession to the picture you had of it while in school?

In school you picture yourself interviewing sports stars and getting that important interview after the game. In reality, until you work your way up in the business, you are much more of a behind-the-scenes participant involved in getting and creating the story for the on-air personalities.

—Sports reporter, 5 years,
Tallahassee, Florida

The broadcasting business is much more difficult than I anticipated. When you start out, you don't have the connections in the community that it takes to get the best footage and the best sound bites. And there are people, usually much more experienced, competing for that same crucial interview.

—News reporter, 4 years, Buffalo, New York

You don't learn in school that broadcasting is a business that is unstructured and yet hierarchical at the same time. The ever-changing events of the world cause you as a reporter to have to be immensely flexible, and yet internally what gets on the air and what does not is controlled with the rigidity of a dictator. Your great work many times never makes it on-air.

—News reporter, 6 years,
Harrisburg, Pennsylvania

. . .

How would you rate your collegiate and graduate courses in preparing you for your profession on a scale of 1 to 10, with 10 being the best?

3. I learned most of the basics from my internship; everything else was trial by fire in the real workplace.

—Weekend sportscaster, 6 years,
Charleston, South Carolina

You learn the basics of reporting in school, but the best teacher is on-the-job training through internships at stations, either during school or in the summer.

—Sports anchor/reporter, 7 years,
Colorado Springs, Colorado

There is a lot of behind-the-scenes work that goes into getting a story or a piece on the air that school does not teach you. Plus you better be able to work with others because it takes cooperation with many different people in many different roles to get a story on-air.

—News reporter, 9 years,
Louisville, Kentucky

THE BIGGEST SURPRISE

What most surprised you about your chosen profession?

How many hours people put in to get the story right. Television is a business based on image and perception, but there are lots of people within the industry who realize how important it is to get the facts right.

—News reporter, 10 years,
Tampa, Florida

How hiring opportunities are determined by factors other than your personal ability as a reporter/broadcaster. Women with less talent are hired over more qualified males because focus groups inform stations that people prefer having the news delivered by attractive women. It is surface, not substance, that counts.

—Sports anchor/reporter, 8 years,
Huntsville, Alabama

How low the pay is for your first ten years in the business. Television is a narcissistic profession, and as long as some young girl or young guy dreams of being on television, there will always be a steady supply of new talent. It becomes pure supply-and-demand economics. Why pay an experienced broadcaster more, when you can replace him or her with someone who will gladly start at one-half the salary.

—Former morning show host, 12 years,
Austin, Texas

HOURS AND ADVANCEMENT

How many hours do you work each week at your career?

Fifty to sixty.

—Weekend sports anchor, 9 years,
Baton Rouge, Louisiana

Forty-five.

—News reporter, 14 years,
Spokane, Washington

I knew that the job required long hours, but there are many big sporting event days when I don't get home until three or four in the morning. The hours (sixty a week) are brutal.

—Sports reporter/anchor, 8 years,
Jacksonville, Florida

. . .

Have you found advancement within your career easy or difficult?

Easy at first, but then I started at a public station in a tiny market, so if you had some on-air talent, it showed. Yet now I am in my third market, and advancement into a top-fifty market is very tough and competitive.

—News anchor/reporter, 9 years,
Champaign, Illinois

Advancement in this business is based on market size. It is a relative term. You can be top dog in a 196th DMA [designated market area] or a beat reporter in a top-fifty DMA. Which one has advanced the most?

—News reporter, 10 years,
Richmond, Virginia

The higher up you go, the harder it gets. It is like pro sports. Lots of guys can play high school ball, fewer can play college ball, and a very few have what it takes to play professional ball.

—News reporter, 12 years,
Salt Lake City, Utah

THE BEST AND THE WORST

What do you spend most of your day doing? Describe a typical day.

Gathering information for stories that have been assigned to me, interviewing sources related to the stories, incorporating videotape footage consistent with the stories, and delivering the stories on-air, as determined by the news directors and assistant news directors.

—News reporter, 7 years, Toledo, Ohio

Analyze the news stories for the day from information received from all available sources, write or supervise the writing of news stories for broadcast, review and correct copy, and deliver the final stories on-air.

—News anchor/reporter, 17 years, Little Rock, Arkansas

The specifics of each day vary based upon the stories being researched or the breaking stories that develop, but the framework for the day remains the same — gather information, create stories from the information gathered, add videotape that best fits and enhances the story, and then present the finished story to the audience.

—Sports anchor/reporter, 6 years, Tulsa, Oklahoma

. . .

What are the best parts of your profession?

Being able to make a difference by presenting a story that truly connects with people and uplifts them or provides them information that improves their lives.

—News reporter, 5 years, Quad Cities, Iowa

Being able to cover, participate in, and be a part of some of the premier sporting events in the world, such as a Superbowl, or a Final Four, or a golf tournament like the Masters.

—Weekend sports anchor, 4 years, Augusta, Georgia

The wide range of fascinating people that you get to meet and interview. Each day is different. New stories are constantly breaking, and your week day to day is constantly evolving. The job is rarely dull.

—Sports anchor/reporter, 12 years, Birmingham, Alabama

. . .

What are the least enjoyable aspects of your profession?

The low pay for the hours that you are expected to work. If you are paid a salary, it sounds adequate when they first hire you, but if you divide that salary by the hours you actually work or are expected to be at certain events, your compensation is extremely low for what the station makes off your efforts.

—Former sports anchor/reporter, 7 years, Lexington, Kentucky

Having to always fight and plead for every expense dollar when you are covering a major event out of your market. The public thinks that we live like kings, only work when we are on-air, and have unlimited expense accounts. The reality is that advertising dollars are down, and the attitude that permeates from the top down in almost every television station is one of constant cost cutting.

—Former weekend sports anchor, 13 years, South Bend, Indiana

The stress of meeting deadlines and working so many long hours. You are lured into the business by the perception of the glamour, the apparent perks, and the dream of making it to the top. But it is difficult to maintain a normal family or social life in this profession when your working hours and those of the rest of the world rarely match up.

—Former news anchor, 17 years, Scranton, Pennsylvania

CHANGES IN THE PROFESSION

What changes do you foresee for your profession?

More consolidation, where larger media companies own more and more stations, and the emphasis on local stories by the in-town stations in each community is reduced.

—News reporter, 8 years, Tucson, Arizona

The stations will be hiring more one-man-band reporters, meaning reporters who also shoot their own video as a cost-cutting move.

—Sports anchor/reporter, 6 years, Greensboro, North Carolina

The role of the television broadcaster is rapidly changing because there will be more use of the internet as a way to both acquire information for stories and deliver news to the audience. The traditional delivery of news at six and eleven will gradually morph into more of a menu-type delivery, where the audience can pick and choose what stories it wishes to see, and when.

—Former sports anchor/reporter, 7 years, Nashville, Tennessee

WOULD YOU DO IT ALL OVER AGAIN?

Do you find your daily job fulfilling?

Yes. Each day is different, and it is rewarding to deliver a story that people in your community find positive.

—Weekend news anchor/reporter, 11 years, Fort Myers, Florida

Day to day, working in broadcasting is a fulfilling job, but long term it is not compatible with any normal life. You are not permitted to connect with your family or your friends within a normal evening or weekend schedule.

—Former sports anchor, 15 years, Greenville, South Carolina

It beats the heck out of most jobs, where you are stuck in an office all day. You meet people you would otherwise never be able to meet, and you are in the middle of events rather than on the outside simply observing them.

—News reporter, 10 years, Columbus, Ohio

. . .

Would you choose the same profession again?

If I were still single, I would choose broadcasting again. But as a married man, I would not recommend it. Too many late nights and long weekends out of town.

—Former sports anchor, 8 years,
Milwaukee, Wisconsin

No. You have to pay your dues in the low-paying markets for too long for the hours you put in. If you want your entire life to be about being a broadcaster, it is an interesting career, but if you want to see your family and have weekends off and be like everyone else, choose another profession.

—News reporter/weekend anchor, 11 years,
Dayton, Ohio

No. The amount you make for the stress you put up with and the hours you put into the job are not worth it until you reach a top-twenty-five market, and by that time you are potentially into your second or third divorce.

—Former sports anchor, 16 years,
Cleveland, Ohio

SO YOU WANT TO BE A WRITER

Most of us picture the profession of writing in terms of the successful author — the Pat Conroys, the Stephen Kings, the John Grishams, the Dan Browns. The reality of the profession is that it is more about the actual craft of writing than about the success that may come from it. None of us can predict success in writing.

Margaret Bennett (author of *Scottish Customs: From the Cradle to the Grave*, among other books) was once quoted in *Publishers Weekly* as saying, "I guess every normal writer has a desire to give birth to a book someday — to become, in fact, an author. Books are . . . a chance at immortality."

Immortality would be nice, but many aspiring writers would be happy simply to make a living. Putting aside the issue of talent, the question is really, what do you want to write about? There are myriad ways to pursue writing as a profession, and depending on your interests, it's as important to be well versed in your subject as it is to be talented in the craft of writing. Unlike in most professions, there are few prerequisites and little training necessary to write a book. But that doesn't mean getting published is easy. On the contrary.

This chapter is focused on becoming a book author, but it includes the thoughts of writers from a range of fields, such as newspaper reporting, songwriting, and screenwriting. Those interested in journalism or non-fiction often begin their writing careers writing articles and stories for newspapers and magazines, either as full-time in-house staff or as free-lancers (independent contractors). Then, having built an expertise in a subject and established their writing credentials, they find it possible to gain the attention of agents and publishers with an idea for a book.

If you want to write fiction, the main advice is to start writing it. Some first try to get published in magazines (writing short stories or other prose), in order to develop their credentials and experience, but this isn't necessary. Successful fiction can emerge from anywhere and from anyone, and few can predict what will sell. This is part of why the art of novel writing is so mysterious and mercurial, and why the publishing industry is so fickle. It is also why even successful novelists have a hard time making a career out of it, and why it's best not to give up your day job too soon.

Through most of human history, books were rare and often sacred objects. Every book had to be written by hand, making each copy extremely valuable. However, it was the practical need to communicate rather than a desire for immortality that produced the development of the written word. Approximately five to six thousand years ago, pictograms (pictures whose meaning is directly related to the image shown; e.g., an image of a snake means snake) were used in Egypt and Mesopotamia. The Chinese conceived the idea of a printed book, *Diamond Sutra* being the first one, dated 868 CE. By 1061 the Chinese had invented movable clay type. However, it was Johannes Gutenberg, a German goldsmith and printer, who revolutionized printing when he invented the first metal movable type press (called the Gutenberg Press) in 1439. In 1455, he printed the world's first book using movable type, the Gutenberg Bible, and for the first time the printed word was made available to the masses. The Gutenberg Press is still considered today to be the most important invention of the second millennium.

With the proliferation of books, literacy grew, and this further spurred

the business of bookselling around the globe. The first important publishing house was that of the Elzevir family in Holland, from the late 1500s
through the 1700s. Printing in America began with printers in Cambridge and Philadelphia. By 1755, there were at least 50 village printing-
bookseller houses scattered throughout the colonies. By 1860 that number
had grown to over 350. In the mid-1800s, such firms as John Wiley and
Sons and House of Harper were formed. At this time, American book publishing split into three categories: the mass dime-novel industry, cheap
reprint companies that supplied home subscription libraries, and a group
of more genteel northeastern houses, which included such names as
George Palmer Putnam, Charles Scribner, and Henry Houghton.

The establishment of international copyrights in 1891 made the prices
of U.S. authors competitive with those of Europeans, and through a pro-
tectionist manufacturing clause, the American printing industry achieved a
new level of prosperity. Books written, printed, and published in American
began to outsell those of European rivals. In 1890 *Publishers Weekly* was
founded as a new trade organization to keep track of sales. Literary agents
had become commonplace by the 1920s. The Book-of-the-Month Club was
started in 1926. After World War II, paperback and, later, chain bookstores
like B. Dalton's and Waldenbooks began to dominate the industry.

The American publishing industry continues to flourish. In 2004 the
number of new titles released reached an all-time high of over 195,000.
The number of new titles decreased by some 18,000 in 2005, only to see
an increase of 3 percent the next year. The odds against becoming the
next bestselling author are staggering. To end up as one of the top one
hundred books of the year, an author's work has to be in the top
1/10,000th percentile of all books sold for that year.

To get your creative work published by a reputable publishing house,
you usually need to follow the traditional, established process. Almost
without exception, the path leads through the office of a literary agent.
Agents have evolved within the publishing industry as the gatekeepers
to the inner sanctum. Like all agents, they work on a commission basis,
usually being paid 15 percent of all monies received by an author. The

principal role of the literary agent is to get a publisher to actually consider your manuscript. Literary agents are part critic and part cheerleader. They have to be excited or moved by your writing before they can enthusiastically recommend it to publishers. And most importantly, they have to conclude that your work is marketable. Agents also know which publishers to approach with which title. While there are publishers who solicit works directly, almost without exception these are "vanity presses," where authors pay to have their own work published.

To get the attention of a literary agent, you typically send a query letter first, which is a one-page summary of your work or idea. Directories of literary agents (which also list the types of books they represent) can be found in your local library. Another effective technique is to examine the acknowledgments of books that are in the same genre as your book. Invariably, the author thanks his or her agent.

Once you are lucky enough to have an agent reply to your query, you will be asked to send your work for their review. With fiction, that means the completed product. With nonfiction, that means a book proposal typically containing an overview, your background as the author, market analysis, chapter summaries, and at least three sample chapters (usually the first three). Book proposals can range from fifty to one hundred pages. So don't start sending those query letters until your work of fiction is complete or your book proposal is ready for delivery.

Robert Louis Stevenson, author of *Treasure Island*, once said, "It takes hard writing to make easy reading." Author W. Somerset Maugham (*Of Human Bondage*) noted, "There are three rules for writing the novel. Unfortunately, no one knows what they are." Walter "Red" Smith, the Pulitzer Prize–winning columnist and sportswriter, stated, "There is nothing to writing. All you do is sit down at a typewriter and open a vein."

So, there you have it. All you need to do to write a successful book is to open up a vein. Easy.

BY THE NUMBERS

EMPLOYMENT LEVELS: According to Bowker, the leading provider of bibliographic information in the United States, there are about two hundred thousand new books published each year in the United States. In addition, there are over a thousand companies that publish over ten thousand different magazines, journals, and tabloids. And this does not include original plays, screenplays, and songs, or newspaper articles, nor all of the content writing now found on the internet. According to the U.S. Bureau of Labor Statistics, the publishing industry employs 660,000 people (this includes all positions within the industry), with 55% working for newspapers, 21.8% for periodicals, and 12.3% for book publishers.

ACADEMIC REQUIREMENTS: There are no specific academic requirements to be a published writer. Individuals from all walks of life and academic backgrounds have been paid for their original writings.

AVERAGE SALARY LEVELS: Book authors are traditionally paid through royalties generated from the sale of their work. However, writers can also be paid a flat fee or a per-word fee (particularly for magazines and newspapers). The vast majority of writers make very little from the sale of their works, but as J. K. Rowling has demonstrated through her Harry Potter series — with an income reported to be over **$1 BILLION** — the sky is the limit.

COLLEGE VS. REALITY

How would you compare the reality of your profession to the picture you had of it while in school?

Most of us picture the profession of writing in terms of the successful author — the Pat Conroys, the Stephen Kings, the John Grishams, the Dan Browns. The reality of the profession is that it is more about the actual craft of writing than about the success that may come from it. None of us can predict success in writing. If we could, Dan Brown's publisher would have done more to keep their author happy rather than push him into the arms of another publisher, who would be the one to reap the $1 billion of revenues from *The Da Vinci Code*. The best you can do is to be committed to your writing.

—**Published writer, 12 years,**
Fort Lauderdale, Florida

I did not attend college or graduate school so I could become a writer. So I did not have a picture of what it would be like. I attended college in hopes of finding a career path. I became a writer because it is what drives me to get up in the morning. I have an insatiable curiosity about most things, and I like doing research. I am eager to find out where my own stories, my own writing, take me.

—**Nonfiction writer, 8 years,**
Charlottesville, Virginia

It has been a much harder road than I thought it would be. I think if people had some idea of how hard it is, how long it takes, they'd think twice. You have to have tremendous perseverance and drive. Each day is a new career. Nothing you've done in the past makes the future any easier. A hit song won't get you your next song. What it might do is get you a faster no.

—**Songwriter, 30 years, Nashville, Tennessee**

. . .

How would you rate your collegiate and graduate courses in preparing you for your profession on a scale of 1 to 10, with 10 being the best?

College doesn't prepare you to be a writer. One's ability to observe life and to give it an interpretation is the key to being a writer. College can assist you in learning about the fundamentals of writing and about the various styles of writing but for the most part writing comes from within.

—**Short story writer, 17 years,**
Lexington, Kentucky

To fully understand the profession of writing, you also need to understand the world of publishing. College does not prepare you for the business side of writing.

—**Nonfiction writer, 8 years,**
Wilmington, North Carolina

Film is a very technical art, and film school exposed me to the process and theory. Graduate school gave me the historiographical background and helped me with my writing. Everything we do in this world is about telling stories.

**—Documentary filmmaker/public historian,
10 years, Nashville, Tennessee**

THE BIGGEST SURPRISE

What most surprised you about your chosen profession?

The pivotal role of the literary agent. It is almost impossible to get inside the doors of the publishing houses without a literary agent. And it is the only client-agent relationship I have ever experienced where it is the agent who calls the shots instead of the client directing the path they want their agent to follow. And for the publishers, it is the best of all worlds. The literary agent can screen the poor examples — the writing, the manuscripts or book proposals that simply are inferior and unmarketable — allowing the editors at the various publishing houses to look only at the cream of the crop. And for this valuable service the publishers pay absolutely nothing. Rather, it is the author who perseveres and eventually rises to the top of the submissions with his or her literary work who is obligated to pay the 15 percent commission to the literary agent.

**—Published author, 5 years,
Providence, Rhode Island**

That you can actually make some money. Generally speaking, journalists don't make a ton of money, but if you work hard, get to a big media market, and produce quality work, I've found that you will be compensated well.

—Sportswriter, 4 years, Cincinnati, Ohio

The fact that being published does not guarantee that the same publisher will even be interested in your next work. You can bet that their standard contract will insist that they have the option on your next work, and your literary agent will use the inclusion of this clause to stroke your ego and tell you that it indicates that the publisher is impressed with your writing. Don't be fooled; the publisher is impressed only with sales results.

**—Published author, 7 years,
New Orleans, Louisiana**

HOURS AND ADVANCEMENT

How many hours do you work each week at your career?

I average fifty hours a week.

**—Newspaper reporter, 9 years,
Savannah, Georgia**

I write six hours a day, four days a week. I then do other things the balance of the week to clear the brain. I do my best to stick to this schedule. That does not mean, however, that I don't lie in bed thinking about the book I am working on, unable to cut the brain off as I write the next several scenes in my head.

—Author, 14 years,
Hilton Head, South Carolina

I am always either working on a new song or thinking about an idea for one. So probably seventy a week.

—Songwriter, 4 years, Austin, Texas

. . .

Have you found advancement within your career easy or difficult?

If advancement equates with getting published, I have found it very hard. You have to write for yourself and hope that one day you can see your work in print.

—Short story writer, 18 years,
Concord, New Hampshire

It depends on how you define advancement. If it means accomplishing the writing, I have advanced quite well. If it means earning lots of money from my writings, I have failed miserably.

—Novelist, 11 years, Rochester, New York

I have been able to secure a literary agent and have a book published within three years of commercial writing. For me, that is advancement.

—Nonfiction writer, 3 years,
Asheville, North Carolina

THE BEST AND THE WORST

What do you spend most of your day doing? Describe a typical day.

Six days a week, I write from 9 AM to 11 AM, then go to the gym or swim laps for an hour, and then go put in eight hours at my job. After a shower and a drink, I write from 10 PM to 1 AM. On Sundays, I spend the day with my wife, but before retiring I usually write at least two hours before calling it a week.

—Nonfiction writer, 7 years,
Las Vegas, Nevada

At least four days a week I meet another songwriter, and we spend the day doing our best to come up with at least one complete original song.

—Songwriter, 15 years, Nashville, Tennessee

I work full-time and write at night. My goal is to have five full pages before I retire for the evening. Not that I will not redraft those five pages many times over at a later date, but as a daily goal, I try to hammer out five pages.

—Aspiring novelist, 2 years,
Natchez, Mississippi

. . .

What are the best parts of your profession?

1) I get to do what I love every day; 2) I get to express myself; 3) I get to

affect people's lives emotionally; 4) I don't have to wear a suit! 5) I make my own hours; 6) I don't have a boss breathing down my neck; and 7) I get holidays and weekends off if I want them.

—Songwriter, 3 years, Nashville, Tennessee

I am able to stay intellectually interested in something other than making a dollar. Writing allows me to follow my own curiosity within a creative format.

**—Nonfiction writer, 10 years,
Fort Worth, Texas**

The process itself. The actual creative side of writing. Starting with a blank page and seeing where I end up. It is as much fun as I have ever had short of sex.

—Writer, 5 years, Virginia Beach, Virginia

. . .

What are the least enjoyable aspects of your profession?

The business side of the profession. It can take two full years between a query letter to an agent and the publication of your book. And that is assuming you can convince a literary agent to represent you, and that you can then write a brilliant book proposal, and that your agent can then find a publisher. Once you receive a deal memo by email, don't celebrate quite yet. It can still take weeks and sometimes months before the contract with your publisher

is signed and that initial partial advance check clears. Oh, and then you have to complete the book, and it better be damn good because when your editor finally gets around to it, and that can be months in and of itself, she (I say she because most editors are women) is going to tear it apart, and so after two years you want to at least end up with something that is fairly representative of what you originally conceived.

—Author, 4 years, Garden City, New York

The lack of a relationship with the editors you deal with. Historically, it was not uncommon for authors and their editors to form a lifelong relationship. In today's world of publishing, the odds are you will never meet your editor, and thanks to email it will be rare if you even have a lengthy phone conversation with him or her. I don't know if it's because editors are overworked and underpaid, and you are just one of a large number of authors that they are dealing with, or if they really don't have any interest in forming a long-term working relationship.

—Author, 10 years, Silver Spring, Maryland

The incredibly short window in which you have for your book to "make it." If you are a first-time author, even if you write a brilliant book, you have to be either a PR genius or just damn lucky to have your work recognized. Your publisher will not do anything out of the ordinary to help you because you do not have a proven record, so it is almost like a pure crapshoot. Plus they have the next book to get out, and they can't dwell on yours unless they know it will be a winner, and they rarely ever know that.

—Nonfiction writer, 4 years,
Sterling Heights, Michigan

CHANGES IN THE PROFESSION

What changes do you foresee for your profession?

Newspapers are in a fight for their survival. With classified ad revenues disappearing because of Craigslist, and with people getting their news off the internet, the days of carving out a career as a traditional newspaper journalist are becoming more and more limited.

—Newspaper journalist, 15 years,
Harrisburg, Pennsylvania

I think there will be more small community theaters emerging, as economically and artistically viable alternatives to the big regional theaters, which will create an opportunity for more original plays.

—Theater director/playwright, 6 years,
Santa Rosa Beach, Florida

The opportunity for first-time authors to become published with a major house will become more and more difficult. In this world of instant gratification, even

the big, established publishing houses are looking for the next big hit, but they are not overly willing to stick their necks out to secure it. Like Hollywood, which continues to remake films that were made decades ago, the publishing world will prefer to risk their advance dollars on proven authors with a sales track record.

—Writer, 10 years, Bellingham, Washington

WOULD YOU DO IT ALL OVER AGAIN?

Do you find your daily job fulfilling?

It is the most rewarding path I have ever followed. Not the most profitable, but by far the most fulfilling.

—Writer, 9 years, Scottsdale, Arizona

If writing is not fulfilling, you would be nuts to do it. The odds of getting published are very remote, and even if you get published, the chance you will make much more beyond your advance is rare.

—Nonfiction writer, 17 years,
Cambridge, Massachusetts

I do not consider writing to be my job. Hopefully I will make enough money from it one day that I can give up my "job." Yet, even with the realization that to live off my royalties is more a dream than a goal, I continue to write. It is who I have become.

—Writer, 5 years,
Lookout Mountain, Tennessee

...

Would you choose the same profession again?

I would indeed, but this time I would not quit my day job while I pursued my literary dreams. Author Cormac McCarthy — who won the 2007 Pulitzer Prize for distinguished fiction by an American author for his novel *The Road* — wrote his first novel, *The Orchard Keeper*, while he was working as an auto mechanic.

—Aspiring novelist, 2 years, New London, Connecticut

I will stick with writing now that I have finally taken the time to pursue it. Even in a world where people are reading fewer books, there is still something almost mystical about being a writer. I was watching an interview with Angelina Jolie where she was asked if the actor who was playing opposite her — in the movie where she portrayed Daniel Pearl's widow — was intimidated by her star power. She answered by saying, "No, I was the one who was intimidated . . . he is a writer, you know."

—Published author, 5 years, Annapolis, Maryland

I just wish I had had the courage to choose this when I was twenty instead of fifty. It is something people can do their entire life and never be bored. You just have to be good enough to continue to be published in some format — books, short stories, magazine articles, etc.

—Writer, 7 years, New Bern, North Carolina

FINDING YOUR DREAM CAREER

If you had all the money you needed, what career would you choose for your life?

Why do we work? Just to pay the bills? To close the next deal?

In our capitalist society, money is the way many people keep score. Who has the highest salary, the biggest house, the coolest car? Who goes to the best schools or travels to the most exotic places? It's easy to get caught up in such comparisons, and as the years fly by, it can begin to feel like a race with no finish line.

Yet aren't our careers and professions about more than just making money? What if we focused on becoming enriched rather than just rich? What if we kept score in comparison not with others but with ourselves, with our own goals and expectations?

In my many months of seeking real-world insights and observations from professionals around the United States, I received hundreds and hundreds of candid and insightful responses. With each questionnaire and interview, I always ended with the same question:

If you had all the money you needed, what career would you choose for your life?

Below are the surprising and interesting answers from fifty individuals, whom I have selected from the responses I received. I have incorporated them into a chart that lists the respondents' current professions, how long they have participated in their chosen careers, and what they named as their dream careers. You may note that some entries are from individuals who do not fall within the career categories in this book. This resulted from the fact that many people I contacted were excited about the book and the impact it could have on the lives of others, and they sent out my questionnaire to friends and associates around the country, regardless of their fields of endeavor. I often received responses from individuals whose professions fell outside the ones I was focused on. The disparity between the chosen professions of some of these individuals and what they held in their minds as their dream career was so surprising that I wanted some of them to become part of the book.

Of the fifty selected responses, only the last eight participants are living their dream careers. Is there a direct correlation between being happy in one's career and participating in a career in the creative arts or in a career where the primary focus is to help others? I will let you draw your own conclusions after reviewing the fifty responses.

Finding Your Dream Career

CURRENT PROFESSION	YEARS OF PROFESSION EXPERIENCE	DREAM CAREER
Mechanical engineer	5	Bookseller
Sports broadcaster	6	Professional surfer
Real estate broker	21	Fishing guide
Software engineer	18	Researcher/developer of prosthetics to improve lifestyles of at-risk children
Ordained minister	6	Goat farmer
Salesperson	38	Historian
Marketing director	12	Professional hunter
Small business manager	7	Office staff member of professional sports team
Teacher	30	Underwater photographer
Attorney	3	Hallmark card shop owner
Real estate broker	8	Professional poker player
Commercial interior designer	7	Event planner
Video game writer	2	Stand-up comedian

THE CAREER CHRONICLES

CURRENT PROFESSION	YEARS OF PROFESSION EXPERIENCE	DREAM CAREER
Marketing/advertising manager	6	Personal trainer
Sales manager of national company	6	Venture capitalist
Certified public accountant	43	Alaskan hunting guide
Health insurance executive	20	Bookstore owner
Portfolio manager	8	Photojournalist
Software engineer	20	Horse caretaker
Landscape architect	7	Travel Channel reporter
Attorney	3	Carpenter
Investment advisor	12	College professor
Sales manager	4	Small-bookstore owner
Oral surgeon	8	Pottery artist
Teacher	6	Fine-art photographer
Engineer	8	Activist for endangered species
Senior vice president in sales	38	Historian

Finding Your Dream Career

CURRENT PROFESSION	YEARS OF PROFESSION EXPERIENCE	DREAM CAREER
Soil scientist	5	Rock star
Public historian	10	Advocate/companion for handicapped children
Attorney	6	BBQ restaurant proprietor
Information technology CEO	41	Restorer of historic homes
Engineer	9	Toy creator
General surgeon	31	National Geographic expeditionist
Geologist	12	Sports car mechanic/restorationist
Accountant	16	Teacher
Electrical engineer	27	National park ranger
Sales director	4	Bookstore owner
Marketing manager	6	Personal trainer
Architect	20	Artist
Global sales manager	40	Golf business entrepreneur
Communications director	5	Writer

CURRENT PROFESSION	YEARS OF PROFESSION EXPERIENCE	DREAM CAREER
Event planner	3	Stand-up comedian
Licensed professional mental health counselor	34	Licensed professional mental health counselor
Songwriter	30	Songwriter
Licensed clinical social worker	5	Licensed clinical social worker
Sportswriter	4	Sportswriter
Theater director/actor	6	Theater director/actor
Speech pathologist	7	Speech pathologist
Pediatric clinical psychologist	2	Pediatric clinical psychologist
Writer	11	Writer

Luckily, *The Career Chronicles* will not be the last by-product that comes to life as a result of my decision to pursue what is my dream career. With the help of talented and persistent literary agents, and after endless rewrites, I now have contractual commitments from publishers for two other manuscripts. For me, having the opportunity to write these books is a testimonial to the proposition that we all are happier in our daily lives when we choose our dream careers, and that if we do not get it right straight out of college, life will afford us the opportunity of another chance.

We just have to be bold enough to take it.

ACKNOWLEDGMENTS

When I first had the idea for *The Career Chronicles*, I underestimated how much collaboration would prove necessary to finally deliver a completed work worthy of the subject matter. Almost no question is more important than *What do I want to do with my life?*

Thanks must first go out to my literary agent, Laurie Markusen, for recognizing the potential of my idea. For an author, Laurie represents the perfect blend of critic and cheerleader, someone unafraid to be honest in her evaluation and yet tireless in her support. She was my initial introduction to the literary world. All aspiring authors should be so fortunate. I gratefully acknowledge that her patience and wisdom have left their permanent imprint on the title, framework, and theme of this work.

I also want to thank all the people at New World Library who worked on this project, but a special appreciation goes out to my editor, Jason Gardner. When I concluded that I needed more interviewees to participate and requested that the book's release date be pushed backed, Jason was understanding, professional, and very supportive, never losing his faith in the project or his belief that there was a broad audience for it. I also want to recognize copyeditor Jeff Campbell for his energetic and most thorough review of the manuscript. Without question his participation improved this book's literary presentation.

Finally, my collective gratitude goes to the hundreds and hundreds of individuals across the United States who took time from their busy schedules to participate in this evolving project, and whose candid observations and insights represent the heart of this book.